Eclipse

Step by Step

Eclipse
Step by Step

Joe Pluta

MC PRESS

Eclipse: Step by Step
A Practical Guide to Becoming Proficient in Eclipse
Joe Pluta

Published by MC Press Online, LP
President: Merrikay B. Lee
Publisher: David M. Uptmor

MC Press Online, LP
Corporate Offices: 125 N. Woodland Trail, Lewisville, TX 75077 USA
Sales and Customer Service: P.O. Box 4300, Big Sandy, TX 75755-4300 USA
Contact 877-226-5394 or *custsrv@mcpressonline.com*

First edition
Second printing—October 2004
ISBN: 1-58347-044-1

Every attempt has been made to provide correct information. However, the publisher and the author do not guarantee the accuracy of the book and do not assume responsibility for information included in or omitted from it.

The following terms are trademarks of International Business Machines Corporation in the United States, other countries, or both: DB2 Universal Database, IBM, the IBM logo, and WebSphere.

Microsoft, Windows, Windows NT, and the Windows logo are trademarks of Microsoft Corporation in the United States, other countries, or both.

Java and all Java-based trademarks are trademarks of Sun Microsystems, Inc. in the United States, other countries, or both.

Other company, product, and service names may be trademarks or service marks of others.

Dedication

*To my wife, Lisa, the only constant in my Universe—and the only person
who knows what FTL means to me.*

Acknowledgments

Once again, I've learned that writing a book is a process, not an act—a *long* process.

Also, I've learned that I am absolutely, certifiably insane, but of course many of you already knew that. However, I can now point to the following adage: Insanity is doing the same thing over and over and expecting different results. In this particular case, this is my second book, and somehow I expected the process to be different. Man, was I wrong.

Writing a book is about having an idea and wanting to express it, and finding out along the way that the "it" that you want to express is changing, and so are you. Unlike a column or an article, which can be written in a span of hours or days, a book is a labor of months or years, and during that time many things change, and so too, must the book.

This is even truer of a book such as this, which is based on a technology, and a new technology at that. And while I want to thank the creators of Eclipse (which is the point of this rather lengthy acknowledgment), I also want to beat them with sticks for the very thing that sets them apart—their unstinting desire to move the product forward and evolve it at breakneck speed.

This evolution is the thing that will make Eclipse and its underlying technologies successful, but it plays havoc on a writer. Even so, I want to thank the Eclipse team, for their unflagging effort, and the greater Eclipse community, for their willingness to answer even the "newbiest" of questions. I want to thank IBM for making this technology public, and I want to thank the third-party developers for embracing and extending the platform in a way I don't think anyone envisioned.

I'd like to thank David Gibbs, the often unsung hero of Midrange.Com, the man who was willing to take on the challenge of reviewing this book. And while he freely admits that he enjoyed taking potshots at the book, his input was invaluable in shaping what you read. Consistency must be attributed to him, lack of it to me.

And, as always, I need to thank Merrikay Lee of MC Press for encouraging me to take on this most daunting and exhilarating of challenges yet again.

Contents

Foreword

Welcome to the first Step by Step book, *Eclipse Step by Step.*

I hope you'll find this book educational and entertaining, as well as a valuable tool. This is the first book that provides an overview of Eclipse and IBM's new Software Widget Toolkit (SWT), and it does so in a unique and powerful way.

Where did the concept for the *Step by Step* books come from? Well, my mentors over at MC Press wanted a set of books that diverged from the traditional "reference manual" products. You know the kind I'm talking about—they go through every possible nuance of a subject in minute detail, making no distinction between something you might use once in your career to something you need every day. These books traditionally break the subject up into sections based on package names or menu options, with hundreds of pages of reference material in the back of the book.

We talked about it, and we agreed that reference books are great for people who already know the subject. But in today's fast-paced data processing environment, things are evolving rapidly, and people need to learn new things, and learn them quickly. My personal experience has always been that the easiest way to learn something in programming is to see somebody else's code. Even better is to have well-commented code. And the best is to have someone walk you through it.

That's what this book is meant to do. Its design is based on the labs I give at various conferences and client sites around the world. My labs are a combination of lecture and mentoring session (which led inevitably to the ungainly name of "lectoring"). Each class starts out with a specific business goal in mind. Compare Java Database

Connectivity (JDBC) and record-level access for business applications, or combine servlets and JavaServer Pages to create a multi-tiered application architecture. I identify my target audience, and then develop a curriculum that meets their needs. The way I do this is to create a test case that will require my students to learn all the things they need to know to reach the original goal. I then walk them through each task required to implement the test case, step by step (thus the title of the book).

In this case, my business goal is to teach you how to use the new Eclipse Integrated Development Environment (IDE) to develop graphical business applications. And since I don't know you personally, I can't assume anything about your knowledge level. That being the case, you'll be able to use this book even if your only knowledge of Java is how to spell it. However, that doesn't mean that Java programmers can't benefit! Even experienced developers can make use of this book, since it will cover three areas that are of crucial interest these days: Eclipse, IBM's SWT, and JDBC. If you've wanted to see a working application using any of those technologies, then this book is for you.

In this book you won't just learn the names of classes and methods or see a list of every menu option along with a brief description. Using this book, you will create, from scratch, a complete functioning application. This book will show you where to get the software, how to install it, how to configure it. It will then focus on those options that you would use in a real production environment—options that will quickly enable you to be productive in Eclipse. It will show you in a real-world environment what steps you would need to take to create a program from scratch, or modify someone else's.

Each step has a checklist of tasks to perform, and each task is documented with screen shots and my editorial comments. Nothing is assumed, nothing left to your imagination. There is no magic in programming, except maybe knowing where to start, and that's where *Step by Step* comes in. The idea of this book is that, once you've finished it, you will understand the subjects well enough to continue learning more on your own.

Because it's that first step that's a doozy.

Joe Pluta
Pluta Brothers Design, Inc.
May 2003

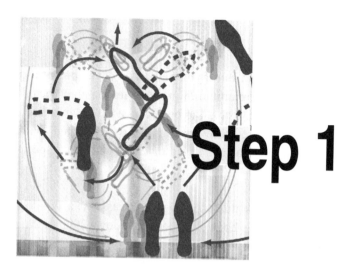

Step 1

Welcome to Eclipse!

Buckle your seat belts, because this is going to be one *fast* ride! In the pages that follow, you're going to learn not one, not two, but three of today's top Java technologies. Not only that, you'll learn how to put them together to create a real business application.

"Wait a minute," you say. "I don't even have Java on my machine!" Well, fear not. This book assumes *nothing*. *Eclipse Step by Step* walks you through downloading and installing every piece of software you need. The only requirement is that your PC has some horsepower and a bit of room on the disk.

The minimum requirements are

> A CPU of 1.5GHz or better
>
> 512MB of RAM
>
> 250MB of disk space.
>
> 1024x768 screen resolution *highly* recommended
>
> Windows machines must have Windows 2000 or better[1]

---

[1]Personally, I use Windows 2000 Professional, and so that is what I recommend. If you have had good luck with Windows XP Professional, you might want to use that instead.

That might look like a hefty machine, but if you plan to do development using today's generation of tools, that's a minimum. I prefer at least a gigabyte of RAM and a 2GHz processor, and I find 1280x1024 to be necessary if I plan to use the tools on a daily basis, but the specs I posted above are enough to get started. With some judicious shopping on the Internet, you can find a machine with those specifications for under $1000 USD.

Where the operating system matters, this book is going to assume a Windows machine. Screenshots throughout the book are from a Windows 2000 machine. However, Eclipse will run on other operating systems, notably Linux and Macintosh, with others available or in development. I've included the latest version of Eclipse for several platforms on the enclosed CD-ROM. Since Eclipse is a very highly integrated environment, there aren't many places where you have to go outside the box, so to speak, and interact directly with the operating system. The only steps that might be different are downloading from the Internet or importing files from the CD. Non-Windows users may need to adjust the scripts for those steps accordingly.

More importantly, Eclipse is designed to take on the look and feel of the host operating system, so non-Windows users will get a different look and feel than Windows users. In fact, there are two Linux versions: one for Motif and one for GTK. This is a fundamental concept of the design philosophy of Software Widget Toolkit (SWT), one of the underlying technologies of Eclipse and one of the topics this book will cover. Also, Eclipse is supported on the Mac only for OS X users; there are currently no plans for an OS 9 implementation.

Several of the Sidesteps show you how to download various pieces of software from the Internet (all software used in this book—other than the Windows operating system—is freely available for download). The browser used in the download steps is Microsoft Internet Explorer version 6. This makes the download process a little different from previous versions of Internet Explorer and significantly different than other browsers. The thing to note is that I instruct the browser to open the files immediately once they are downloaded rather than save them to a folder on my disk drive. This is more of a convenience rather than a recommended practice. Whatever your current practices are for downloading software, please follow them. In particular, if you are working on a company machine, please follow your corporate security procedures.

Windows and Linux users need a Java virtual machine (JVM)—Sidestep 1 will help you download one if you do not already have one. Macintosh users have their own JVM, so they don't need this particular step. I've also included the SQL engine that the exercises use, HSQLDB. I like HSQLDB because it's a pure Java implementation, so it will run anywhere you have a JVM, with no additional installation considerations.

Finally, because some people may prefer other SQL engines or might prefer Swing over SWT, I've included Sidesteps on those particular topics to help you adapt these exercises to those technologies. If the previous sentence made no sense, then you probably don't have to worry about those Sidesteps!

How it works

The Step by Step books are very simple in format. The entire book is broken down into sequential steps. They are meant to be followed in order. Each Step will have a checklist. The checklist will look something like this:

✔ **Here is your step checklist:**

❏ 1.1(a) Place toothpaste on the toothbrush 1

❏ 1.1(b) Brush teeth vigorously for two minutes 2

(. . .)

The number on the left will refer to the step (1.1, 1.2, 2.1, and so on) and the task within that step (a, b, c, . . .). The page number on the right refers to the page number where that particular task can be found.

Each step will start on a new page and will have a heading and a goal statement. There may be a paragraph or two of additional information as well. Each task will have detailed instructions and one or more associated illustrations (occasionally several tasks will refer to the same image, for example when filling out the fields of a dialog box).

Some of the steps may seem very simple, especially if you already have some experience in a given area, but I wanted to be sure not to leave anything out. If you follow all the steps to the letter, by the time you finish the book you will have completed the goal of creating a business application using Eclipse, SWT, and JDBC.

Step 1.1—Brushing your teeth

> **GOAL**
>
> In this step,
> you will brush your teeth.

Note: If you have dentures, please use the dentures SideStep.

❑ **1.1(a) Place toothpaste on the toothbrush**

Figure 1.1: Putting toothpaste on the toothbrush.

You'll notice that if there are several ways to do something (such as open a file), I may do it differently at different places in the book. This is to give you some exposure to the many ways Eclipse allows you to do things. Eventually you'll develop your own preferences as to how to do these things.

What I'll cover

Eclipse

The first big topic in the book is Eclipse. Indeed, that's probably the reason you bought the book—to learn how to use Eclipse. Eclipse is a huge application—a set of applications, really—and since it's an Open Source project, it's constantly evolving and growing. You'd literally need thousands of pages of documentation to keep up with everything, but as with all such applications, you will use only a small part of the entire application in your day-to-day activities.

Without any features added, Eclipse doesn't do much of anything. It is really just a common framework onto which you can attach tools. However, Eclipse comes with a couple of standard features. One is the Plug-In Development Environment (PDE), which we won't be covering in this book. The other is the Java Development Tooling, or JDT, which is our focus. The JDT is the standard Eclipse Java IDE.

The primary tasks for any IDE are managing, editing, compiling, and debugging code. In this book, you will:

1. Create a Java project

2. Enter source code and edit it

3. "Compile," run, and debug an application

I put the word compile in quotes, because the JDT automatically compiles source when you save it. It's important to remember, though, that Eclipse is not simply about Java development. The Java Development Tooling feature is just one of many features that can be added to Eclipse.

As you read this, people are working all over the world adding other features to Eclipse. These plug-ins will add all sorts of new capabilities, from support for additional languages to extra options such as Google searches or even an MP3 player.[2]

---

[2]For more information on plug-ins, try *eclipse-plugins.2y.net/eclipse/plugins.jsp.*

And the wonderful thing about it is that if these features are written in the spirit of the Eclipse framework, then it will be easy for you to learn to use them, because you will already be familiar with Eclipse. In this book, you will learn the features that all Eclipse applications share and the common operations and actions that can be used with any well-designed Eclipse feature.

The Java Development Tools (or JDT)

While I will teach you the common aspects of the Eclipse environment, I do want this to be productive, and so most of your time in this book will be spent in the JDT. The JDT is as close to a "base plug-in" as you will get; the developers of Eclipse put a lot of work into the JDT. Each new release of Eclipse includes an updated JDT, and I think the JDT is one of the primary testing grounds for the SWT (which I'll get to in a moment).

The JDT is IBM's replacement for the Visual Age for Java IDE (which was, in my opinion, the best Java IDE available). It's no coincidence that one of the primary teams behind Eclipse and the JDT is a company called Object Technology Inc. (OTI), the same folks who brought you Visual Age for Java. This is a very bright, very innovative group of folks.

The Standard Widget Toolkit (or SWT)

One of the biggest innovations from the Eclipse team, an innovation that grew out of OTI's long experience with graphical interface design, is the Standard Widget Toolkit or SWT.

The JDT is the next generation of Visual Age for Java. One of the problems with VAJ was that it was pretty platform-specific. That was because it used a very complex and sophisticated UI. The OTI team figured out a way of combining the run-anywhere nature of Java with the performance of native GUI routines. While there is great debate over the architecture of this approach, there is no doubt that the SWT API allows the creation of some very powerful application code.

The SWT is different from other Java packages. First off, it requires a native piece—a DLL in Windows, a shared library in Linux. SWT won't run unless that piece is available. Second, much of the SWT has been designed to keep as small a footprint as possible. This has been done with the thought in mind that any program written for a larger machine should be able to be run on a portable. Thus SWT is designed to run on machines using Windows CE or similar micro edition operating systems.

Note: If you're not comfortable using SWT, I've included an alternate set of Swing-based programs. There's nothing in the text to support them, and they'll be fairly different from Swing in several areas, so you might have to adjust your text accordingly of you use. Even if you don't use the Swing examples, you can compare them with the SWT code.

JDBC and HSQLDB

Finally, once you've learned how to talk to the user via SWT (or Swing if you're so inclined), you need to talk to a database. Without this capability, a business program is largely useless. Step 10 deals specifically with accessing the database.

I've used HSQLDB, an Open Source 100% Pure Java SQL database engine, as the underlying database for this book. I did it because, of the many SQL engines I've worked with, HSQLDB required the least work during initial setup. Basically, it was unzip and go. However, you may want to use a different database. I've included instructions on some of the more popular free databases, such as PostGreSQL.

So, if you're ready, it's time to get started. Enjoy!

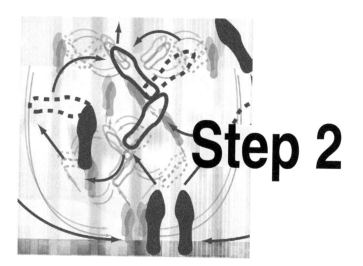

Step 2

Installing Eclipse

Before you install Eclipse, your system must meet a few hardware and software prerequisites, and a couple of additional downloads are recommended. The hardware prerequisites for your machine were outlined in Step 1. The only additional requirements are the software—you must have a Java runtime environment and a ZIP file utility.

If you have a Macintosh, your Java runtime is built in. For Windows or Linux machines, you need to download one, but they are readily available. To do this, go to SideStep 1. Also, if you are running Microsoft Windows, I highly suggest the WinZip utility. If you do not already have this program, SideStep 2 shows you how to get it.

Finally, you can either use the Eclipse SDK version included on the CD-ROM or download the latest version. The release of this book was timed to include the final release of version 2.1 of Eclipse, released on March 28, 2003. Based on when you are reading this book, you may choose to download a later release rather than use the included software. In general, I'd say the CD version will be fine for at least a year (that is, until March 2004). After that (or if you enjoy seeing new features), I would recommend downloading a newer version. Information on downloading Eclipse from the Eclipse Web site is available in SideStep 3.

Note: Just remember that if you do download a newer version, chances are that there will be minor changes to some of the screens.

Once you've met these initial requirements and decided on which Eclipse version to use, you can continue on.

The following checklist can be used to make sure you have completed all the activities for this step.

Step 2.1—Extract Eclipse

> ## GOAL
>
> **In this step, you will install the Eclipse IDE from its ZIP file, either the one included on the CD-ROM or the one you downloaded in SideStep 3.**

Note: The next task assumes a Windows machine with WinZip installed. If you are not running Windows, or if you use another ZIP file extraction program, use the utility of your choice to extract all the files in the ZIP file into the folder C:\Program Files\eclipse (be sure to use subfolders), and then skip to Step 2.2.

    If you don't want to use the folder name C:\Program Files\eclipse, feel free to use your own and modify the instructions that follow accordingly.

❑ **2.1(a) Using the Windows Start button, start WinZip.**

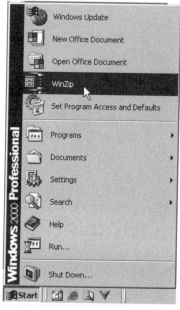

Figure 2.1: Start WinZip from the Windows Start menu.

❑ **2.1(b) Click the Open button.**

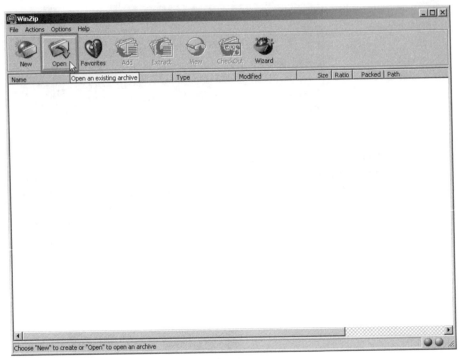

Figure 2.2: Open a file using the Open button.

Now, you need to select the file. I will walk you through the steps to open the ZIP file included on the CD-ROM. If, however, you've downloaded a different version of Eclipse using SideStep 3, you'll need to navigate to that file instead.

❏ **2.1(c) Select your CD-ROM drive.**

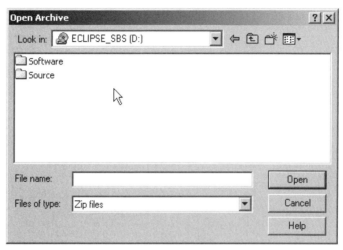

Figure 2.3: Select your CD-ROM drive.

❏ **2.1(d) Open the Software folder.**

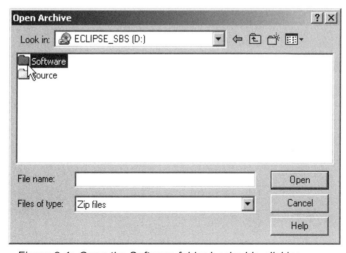

Figure 2.4: Open the Software folder by double-clicking.

❏ **2.1(e) Open the Eclipse folder.**

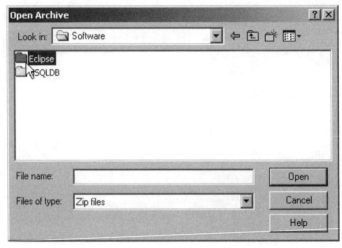

Figure 2.5: Open the Eclipse folder by double-clicking.

❏ **2.1(f) Open the Eclipse SDK ZIP file.**

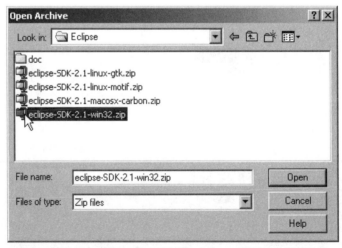

Figure 2.6: Open the SDK ZIP file, eclipse-SDK-2.1-win32.zip, by double-clicking.

You will see the ZIP file contents as shown in Figure 2.7.

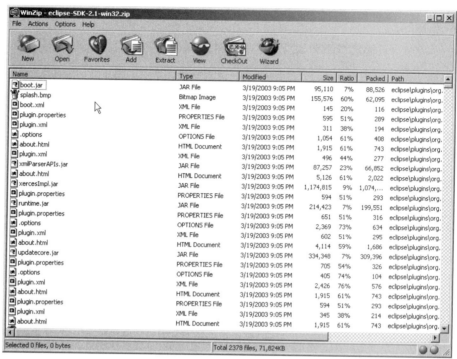

Figure 2.7: *The WinZip display shown when you open the downloaded SDK ZIP file.*

❑ 2.1(g) Click the Extract button.

Clicking the Extract button will bring up a dialog box that allows you to select a directory to install the ZIP contents into. This dialog will look like the one in Figure 2.9.

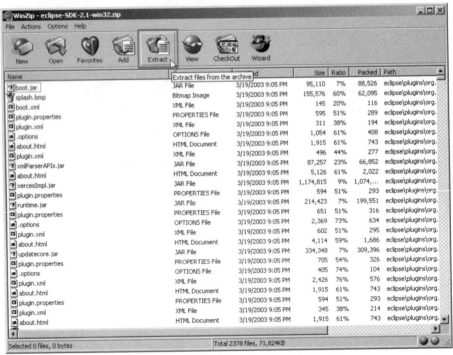

Figure 2.8: Click the Extract button to begin installing the SDK files.

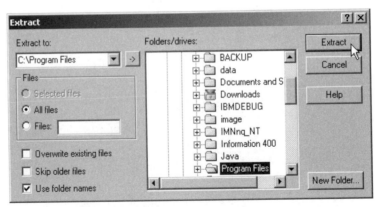

Figure 2.9: The WinZip extraction dialog.

You now need to decide where to install this software. I prefer to use "C:\Program Files", because the IDE is after all a program. Everything in the ZIP file is actually in a folder called "eclipse" or one of its subfolders, so after you've finished, you'll see a folder named "eclipse" under "C:\Program Files". Also be sure that the checkbox marked "Use folder names" is checked; otherwise the extract process will not build the required directory structure.

Note: You will need to know the name of this folder for later Steps, particularly Step 4, so I'm going to have you save it.

☐ **2.1(h) Save the directory name as $ECLIPSEINST: _____.**

☐ **2.1(i) Enter the value of $ECLIPSEINST as the directory and click Extract.**

A status dialog like the one in Figure 2.10 will come up to show you the progress of the extraction.

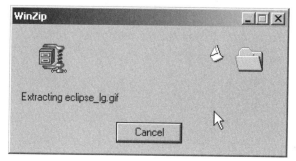

Figure 2.10: The WinZip extraction status display.

Once this finishes, you have successfully installed Eclipse. Time to run it. First, close WinZip, either by selecting the File menu and then selecting the Exit option or by clicking on the X in the upper right corner of the WinZip window.

❑ **2.1(j) Close WinZip.**

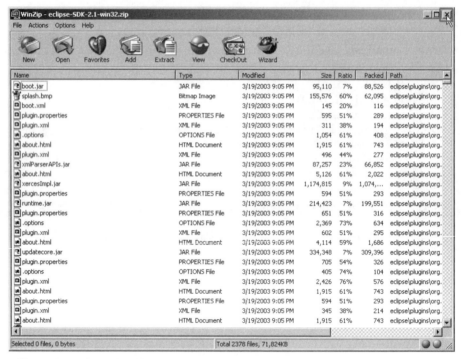

Figure 2.11: Close WinZip by using the X button.

Step 2.2—Run Eclipse

GOAL

In this step, you will run the Eclipse IDE.

☐ 2.2(a) Locate the IDE.

Unlike many Windows programs, Eclipse does not automatically add an option to the Start button. Instead, to start the IDE, you first need to navigate to the correct folder using Windows Explorer, as shown in Figure 2.12.

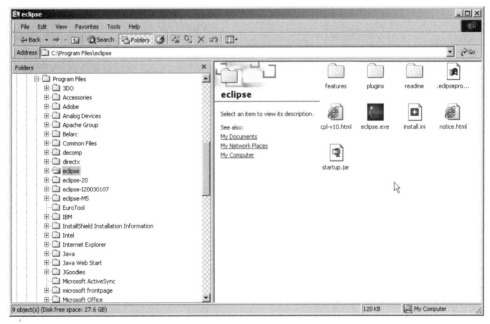

Figure 2.12: The Eclipse folder, indicating the launch icon for the IDE.

At this point, you may want to make a shortcut icon that you can place either on your desktop or in your start menu. Personally, I use the Microsoft Office quick launcher. I just drop the icon on the bar and it's there for me whenever I need it.

❑ **2.2(b) Right-click the IDE icon and select Create Shortcut.**

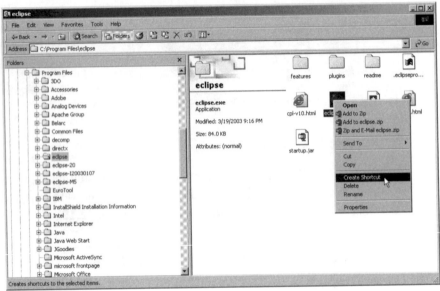

Figure 2.13: Use the pop-up menu to create a shortcut for the IDE icon.

A new icon will appear, which will look exactly like the IDE icon, but with an arrow on the bottom left indicating that this is a shortcut. You can now move this shortcut icon wherever you want to allow easy access to the program.

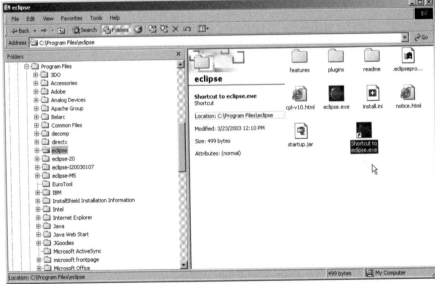

Figure 2.14: The Eclipse folder, indicating the launch icon for the IDE.

❑ 2.2(c) Start the IDE.

eclipse.exe

Note: Once you have located the Eclipse folder, double click on the IDE icon, shown on the left. You can also use the shortcut icon you created in Step 2.2(d). You will see the small window shown in Figure 2.15, followed by the splash screen in Figure 2.16. The first window only appears the first time you start Eclipse after the install, but the splash screen appears every time.

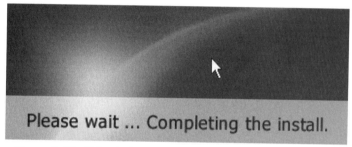

Figure 2.15: This window is shown only the first time you launch Eclipse.

Figure 2.16: The startup screen for the Eclipse IDE.

❑ **2.2(d) Wait for the IDE workbench to appear.**

On the machine used for this book, a 1.6GHz Pentium 4, the splash screen stayed up for about 12 seconds. Then the screen shown in Figure 2.17 appeared.

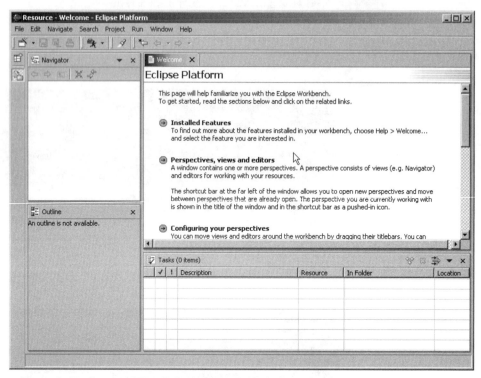

Figure 2.17: Success! The Eclipse IDE in its default configuration!

Step 3

Introducing the workbench

Everything in Eclipse is done through the workbench. The workbench is sort of your view on the world. In this step, I'm going to introduce you to it.

First, I'll point out the different parts of the workbench. Then I'll show you the Eclipse Workbench User Guide, an in-depth guide to the features of the workbench. This is an excellent reference document.

In the next step, we will learn more about the components and how to use them.

✔ **Here is your step checklist:**

Introduction

First, I'll review the basic components of the Eclipse IDE workbench. Figure 3.1 shows the workbench with the various pieces broken apart. If your screen doesn't resemble the one shown (not exploded, of course), then please execute the actions in Step 3.1 to get to the initial welcome display.

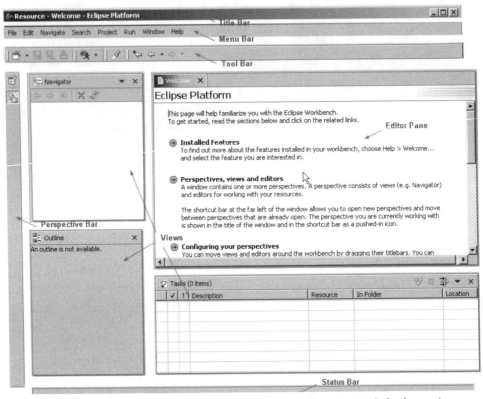

Figure 3.1: The Eclipse IDE Workbench, with its individual components broken out.

The basic workbench, no matter what perspective you use, consists of a group of panels (or panes) surrounded by a group of bars. A specific collection of panels is known as a *perspective*. In this particular perspective, you'll notice a Navigator view in the upper left panel. Typically, this sort of panel is used to group all the components of your project. The components are referred to as *resources*.

The default perspective is the Resource perspective, which basically treats all resources as text files.

The bars

The bars tend to stay the same from one perspective to the next. While you can customize the appearance and content of the bars, the bars themselves tend to always be available and in the same locations.

1. Title Bar: This is the standard Windows title bar (or whatever operating system you happen to be running Eclipse under). The title bar always displays the name of the current perspective.

2. Menu Bar: This is the overall Eclipse menu bar, which allows you to do all manner of general tasks. The available options in this menu will also change based on the resource currently selected.

3. Tool Bar: This is the overall Eclipse tool bar, which also allows you to perform both general tasks and specific tasks for selected items.

4. Perspective Bar: The perspective bar allows you to switch quickly between open perspectives or to open new perspectives.

5. Status Bar: This line typically displays information about the selected item, although it can contain additional information depending on the task you're currently performing. For example, when you're in a text editor, the status bar might show the current position within the document.

The panels

There are two types of panels: views and editors.

1. Views: Views show groups of related objects. In a typical display (although this is by no means required), the upper left hand panel will show a Navigator view.

2. Editors: Editors are just what the name implies: tools to edit documents. These documents can be program source or runtime configurations—basically, anything that can be edited.

Views are lists of items. They can be the resources in a project; in which case the view is generally called a Navigator view. Another view type is the task list, which contains to-do items, such as current syntax errors. A third view type is the attribute view, which might show either the properties or the outline of a selected item in the navigator view. The number of views continues to grow as third-party developers create more and more plug-ins. However, in this book you'll only need to learn the basic views shipped with the Eclipse product itself.

Note that some views come with their own toolbars. These toolbars are in addition to the main Eclipse tool bar and provide additional, view-specific functions.

As opposed to views, which can be rather free-form, editors are quite focused. They generally provide context-sensitive, syntax-aware editing for the selected resource. While the open-source Eclipse project really only has a single editor (the Java editor), IBM has written many more editors, and many of these are available in the WebSphere Development Studio client. They include editors for everything from RPG to COBOL, from JavaServer Pages to Cascaded Style Sheets.

There are also a number of third-party editors, ranging from C and C++ to COBOL. Editors for languages you might not normally hear about, such as Eiffel and AspectJ, are being developed, as well as more popular names such as Pascal and Python.

Step 3.1—Getting to the welcome display

GOAL

**In this step, you will display
the initial Eclipse Welcome screen.**

Note: When you finished Chapter 2, your workbench should have been left looking like what is shown in Figure 3.2. If it is, skip to step 3.2. If not, execute the
commands in this step.

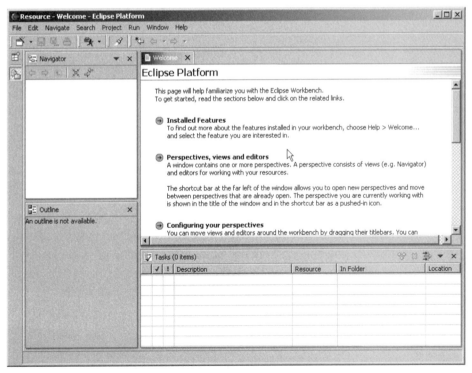

Figure 3.2: The Welcome Page for Eclipse.

☐ **3.1(a) From the menu bar, select Window/Close All Perspectives.**

Select the Window menu on the menu bar. The Window menu appears. Select the Close All Perspectives option, as shown in Figure 3.3.

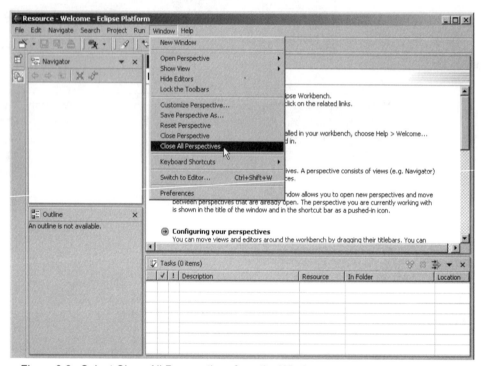

Figure 3.3: Select Close All Perspectives from the Window menu.

From now on, when I want you to select a menu and then execute an option (perhaps by selecting options from one or more intervening submenus), I will show the series of selections separated by slashes, like this:

Select Window/Close All Perspectives

Your workbench will change to what is shown in Figure 3.4.

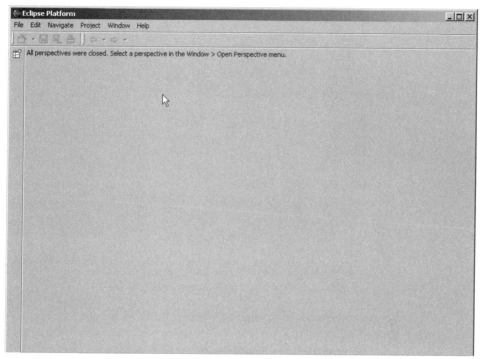

Figure 3.4: A completely empty workbench.

❏ 3.1(b) From the menu bar, select Window/Open Perspective/Resource.

Select Window on the menu bar. Note that the Open Perspective option has a small triangle on the right (Open Perspective ▶). The triangle means that when you select the Open Perspective option, a submenu appears, as shown in Figure 3.5 on the following page. Select Resource from the submenu.

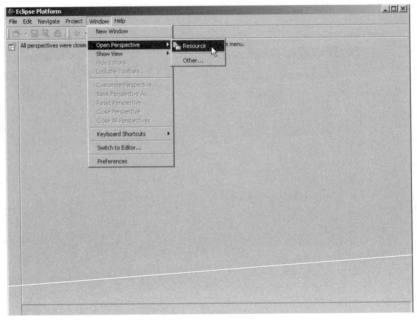

Figure 3.5: Opening the Resource persepective.

Your workbench will change to what is shown in Figure 3.6.

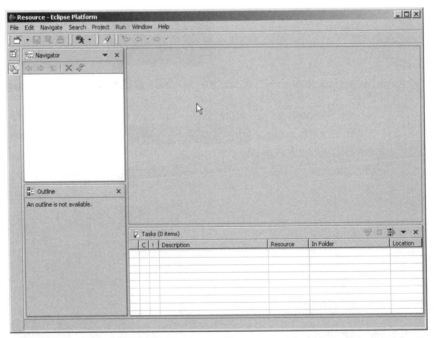

Figure 3.6: An empty Resource perspective.

❑ 3.1(c) From the menu bar, select Help/Welcome. . .

From the Help menu, select Welcome. . . Note the ellipsis dots (. . .) after the word "Welcome". The dots indicate that the option will bring up a wizard. Wizards are a very powerful feature that you'll see more frequently in the following pages.

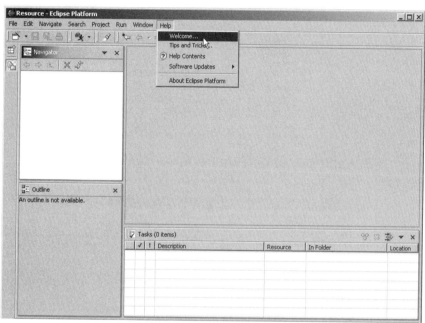

Figure 3.7: Select Welcome . . from the Help menu.

❑ 3.1(d) From the Welcome wizard, select Eclipse Platform and press OK.

A wizard is a series of one or more panels that walk you through the selections and inputs you need to make to use some feature of Eclipse. The Welcome wizard contains only one panel, shown in Figure 3.8.

Figure 3.8: The Welcome wizard.

Step 3.2—Eclipse's own tutorial

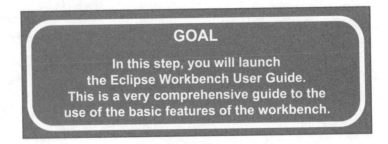

GOAL

In this step, you will launch
the Eclipse Workbench User Guide.
This is a very comprehensive guide to the
use of the basic features of the workbench.

❑ **3.2(a) Click the scroll bar in the editor pane.**

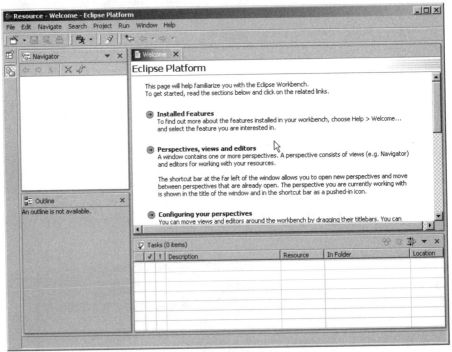

Figure 3.9: The Welcome Page for the Eclipse Platform.

❏ **3.2(b) Drag the scroll bar to the bottom of the page.**

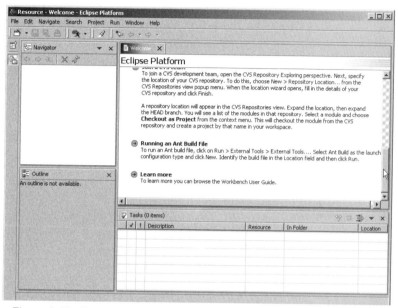

Figure 3.10: The bottom of the Welcome Page for the Eclipse Platform.

❏ **3.2(c) Click the hyperlink entitled Workbench User Guide.**

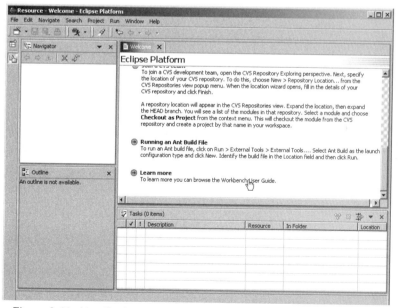

Figure 3.11: Use the hyperlink to bring up the User Guide.

At this point, a new window will pop up looking like the one shown in Figure 3.12.

❏ **3.2(d) Click the hyperlink entitled Getting Started.**

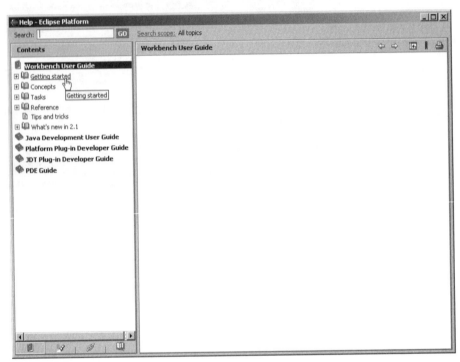

Figure 3.12: The Eclipse User Guide.

Getting Started will take you to a section that includes a very nice high-level tutorial on Eclipse and the IDE. It covers most features of Eclipse, but more from a reference standpoint than as a user's guide. There are other sections in the tutorial, which cover other portions of Eclipse. It's an excellent companion piece to this guided tour.

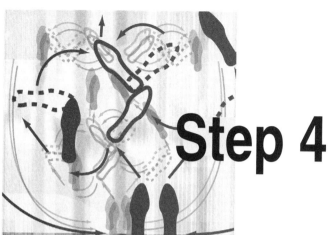

Step 4

The Resource perspective

In the last chapter, I noted that everything in Eclipse is done through the workbench, your view of the world. However, that view can be customized and personalized—fine-tuned to exactly what you need when you need it. That's the job of the perspective and its components: the views and editors.

In this step, you will use the various components of the Resource perspective.

✔ Here is your step checklist:

Review

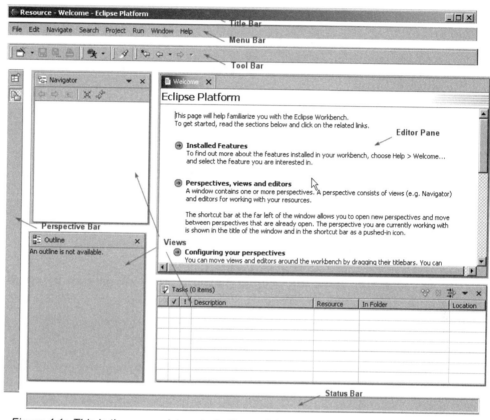

Figure 4.1: This is the same picture as in Figure 3.1.

Figure 4.1 is the same as Figure 3.1. It shows an "exploded" view of the workbench. As I noted in Step 3, this happens to be the default perspective, the Resource perspective, which treats all resources as text files.

Interestingly enough, for this step you will remain entirely within the central section of the workbench, the views. The way Eclipse is designed, you can usually do the majority of your work without ever having to use the main menu bar or tool bar. In this step, I'll walk you through creating a trivial test project.

Step 4.1—Close the Welcome window

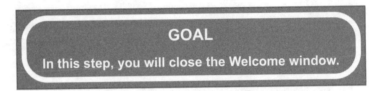

GOAL

In this step, you will close the Welcome window.

Let's get rid of the Welcome panel. You may have noticed that the Welcome window is in the location I told you was normally used for editors. In fact, the Welcome display is technically an editor. It's a read-only editor; you can't actually change the contents of the window. But it displays many of the characteristics of other editor panels, including the fact that it has a small tab that displays at the top of the editor panel.

When you have multiple resources open for editing, you will see more than one of these tabs. You will see in later steps that you can use the tabs for manipulating the editors in many ways. But for now, you're just going to use the "close" capability.

❑ **4.1(a) Close the Eclipse Platform Welcome window by clicking on the X on its tab.**

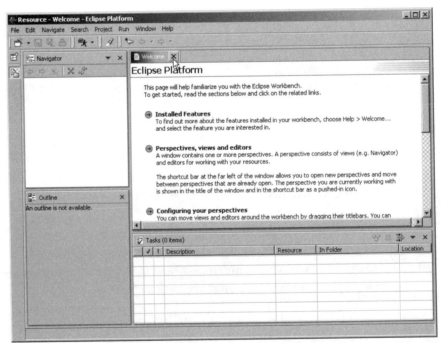

Figure 4.2: Close the Welcome panel by clicking on the X.

Step 4.2—Create a project

> ## GOAL
>
> **In this step, you will create
> a simple project. This action will
> introduce you to the concepts of views and
> actions as well as projects, folders, and resources.**

After having closed the Welcome panel in step 4.1, your workbench should look like
the one shown in Figure 4.3.

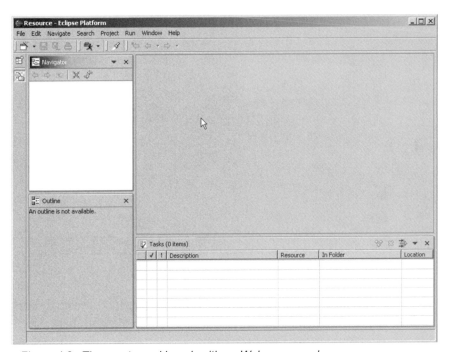

Figure 4.3: The empty workbench with no Welcome panel.

Now you need to create a project. Most resource-oriented tasks are done with a Navigator view. The Navigator view is typically in the upper left pane of the perspective, and it shows all the resources in your project grouped in a logical way.

The more specific your perspective is, the more it knows about your resources and the more it can manage your views. The Navigator view in the Resource perspective knows almost nothing about the resources; it knows only projects, folders, and files. So when you create a project and resources, that's really all you'll be doing: creating folders and files. But first, let's create a project.

❏ **4.2(a) Position your cursor in the Navigator pane and right-click.**

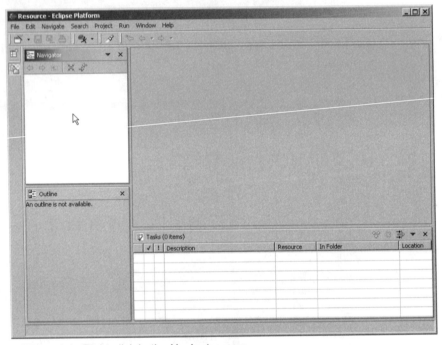

Figure 4.4: Right-click in the Navigator pane.

This is the typical manner of bringing up a context-sensitive menu. Move your cursor into a panel (either a view or an editor) and right-click. Each panel has its own context-sensitive menu (or none).

In this case, there are no items to click on, so you'll bring up a sort of default menu for that view. If there were one or more items selected in the view, the menu would be contain options relevant to the selected item or items.

❏ 4.2(b) Select New/Project . . .

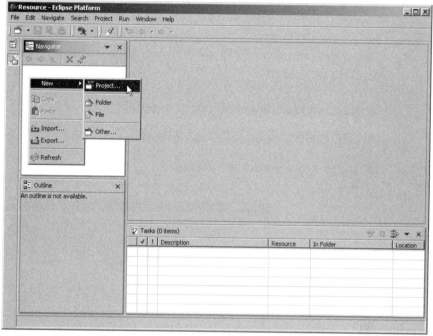

Figure 4.5: Select the New submenu, then the Project… option.

Okay, now I'll go on to the New Project wizard.

Figure 4.6: The New Project wizard is a typical wizard.

The New Project wizard as shown in Figure 4.6 is typical of the many wizards in
Eclipse. As mentioned in Step 3, a wizard is a set of one or more panels that walk
you through the selections and inputs you need to make to accomplish some task
such as the definition of an item. Instead of having to create a project and then modify its attributes, you simply walk through a set of forms that prompt you for all the
pertinent information.

❑ **4.2(c) In the left pane, select Simple.**

❑ **4.2(d) In the right pane, select Project.**

❑ **4.2(e) Click the Next> button.**

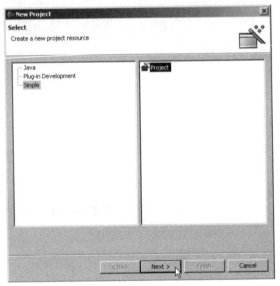

*Figure 4.7: Select the options to create a "Simple"
project.*

You probably noticed that there are many other kinds of projects to create besides the
Simple project I've told you to build. You'll learn more about other project types in
later steps. For now, the Simple project is all you need.

Clicking the Next> button brings up, logically enough, the next panel in the wizard. Normally, a wizard allows you to move back and forth between the various panels by clicking the <Back and Next> buttons. The last page will have a Finish button, which will then execute the action. (Sometimes there will be a Finish button on pages prior to the last, creating a shortcut that bypasses some of the panels.)

❑ **4.2(f) Type 'Simple Project' in the Project name field and press Finish.**

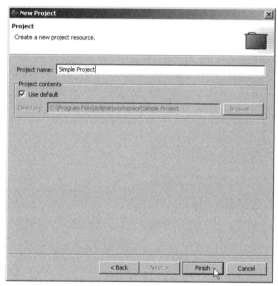

Figure 4.8: Type in the project name ("Simple Project") and press the Finish button.

This will create the project. Depending on the speed of your machine, you may or may not be able to read the progress dialog that pops up. On my machine, it's gone so fast that I can't even capture it.

You should now see the screen shown in Figure 4.9.

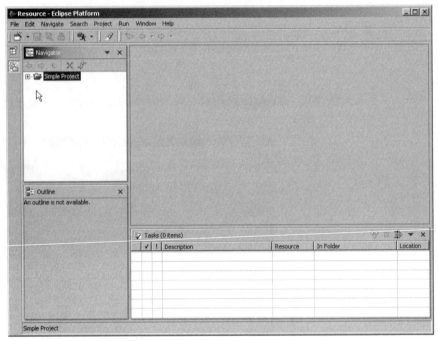

Figure 4.9: Congratulations! You have created a project named Simple Project.

The interesting thing about this is that the project looks as if it already has something in it. The little "plus sign" to the left of the project indicates that an item can be expanded. So let's expand it, shall we?

❏ **4.2(g) Expand Simple Project by clicking on the plus sign.**

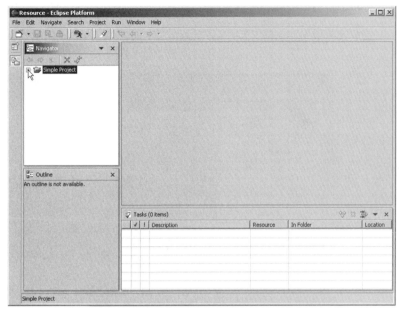

Figure 4.10: Clicking on the plus sign will expand the project.

And what is this? A file called .project? What could be in there?

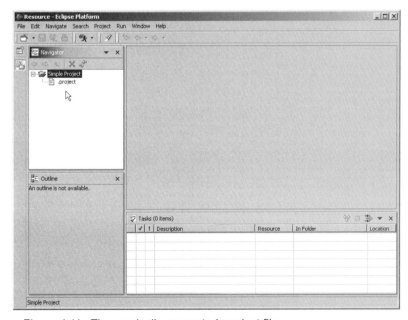

Figure 4.11: The magically generated .project file.

Well, being the curious type of folks we are, we could find out. The easiest way to see the contents of an item are to double-click on it. Let's do that.

❑ **4.2(h) Double-click on .project to open it in the default editor.**

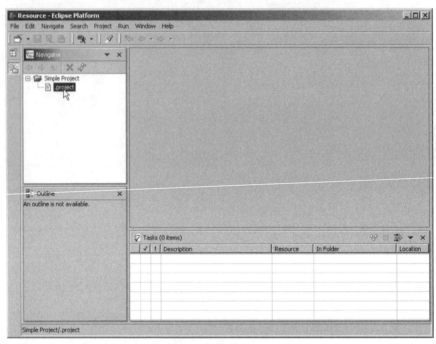

Figure 4.12: Double-click on the .project file to open it in an editor.

And this is the result:

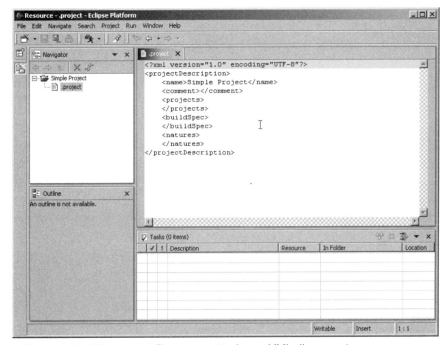

Figure 4.13: The .project file turns out to be an XML diocument.

This is something called a *project description*. This is where Eclipse gets a little bit convoluted, but very powerful. The various elements of the project description are all available within the workbench itself. Therefore, you can now build your own commands to access this information and do your own thing.

Some of the pre-defined features are the buildSpec and natures elements. The buildSpec defines the instructions used to build the project, while the natures element can be used to customize the project in various ways. Both of these are well outside the scope of this particular document; they will be covered in more detail in the book *Eclipse Plug-Ins, Step by Step*.

Get used to the concept, though, of Eclipse creating XML files under the covers. The more you use Eclipse and the more specific your plug-ins get, the more XML files you will see. For example, the IBM plug-ins that are used for some of their more advanced development tools generate many different kinds of XML files.

Step 4.3—Create a Resource

GOAL

In this step, you will create
a resource—in this case, a simple text file.

As I noted earlier, the Resource view is quite generic and really can't be used for anything other than gathering and arranging text documents. However, by creating a few files and moving them around, I can show you the basics of manipulating resources within the workbench.

❑ **4.3(a) Right-click on Simple Project and select New/File . . .**

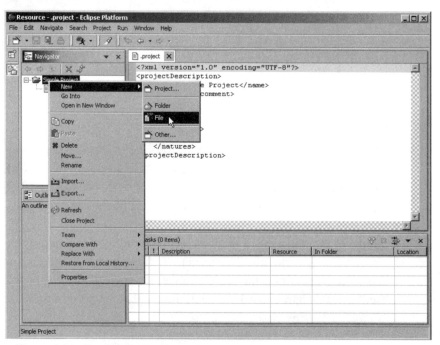

Figure 4.14: For Simple Project, select New/File . . .

Since the File. . . option ends in an ellipsis (. . .), you might expect that the next thing you'll see is a wizard, and you would be correct. You'll see the New File wizard, as shown in Figure 4.15.

❑ **4.3(b) Enter 'Step List.txt' in the File name: field and click Finish.**

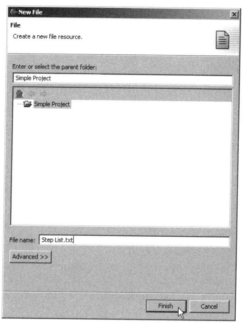

Figure 4.15: The New File wizard, which prompts you for the name of the new file.

When the wizard completes, you'll be brought back to the workbench, and you'll see that a file, Step List.txt, has been added to Simple Project, as shown in Figure 4.16.

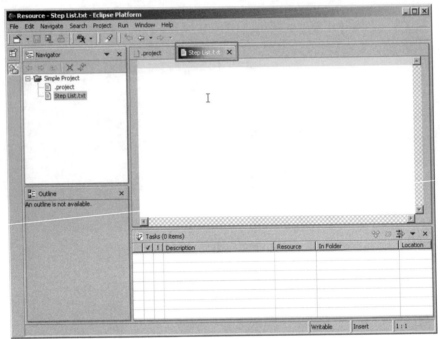

Figure 4.16: The workbench shows the new file, as well as an editor for it.

You'll notice that a new tab appears in the editor pane for Step List.txt. This tab is highlighted, and the tab for .project is no longer highlighted. This indicates that Step List.txt is the active file. Normally, you'll only have one active file in the editor pane at a time. I'll show you later how to change that. For now, it's just time to enter the data for the file.

❏ **4.3(c) Enter the source as shown.**

```
Step 1 - Enter a Program
Step 2 - Run and Debug
Step 3 - Add a User Interface
Step 4 - Add a Database
```

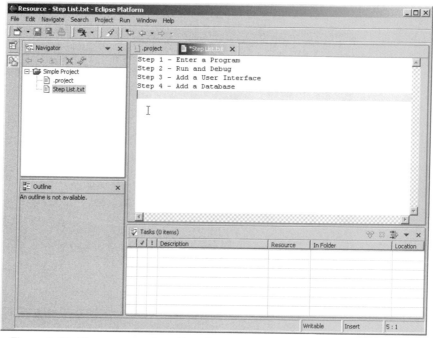

Figure 4.17: The source entered into Step List.txt.

Once you start entering data, you'll notice that the editor tab for this file has an asterisk next to the file name. The asterisk indicates that changes have occurred in this file since the last time it was saved. The only way to make the asterisk go away is by saving the affected file.

Saving items is a fairly consistent, straightforward process. The easiest way is to right-click in the editor pane for that file, then select Save.[1]

---

[1]As is often the case in Eclipse, there are many ways to do the same thing. In this case, you could use the save icon on the toolbar, or the File/Save. . . option from the main menu. I'll show you some of these alternate techniques in other steps of the book.

❑ **4.3(d) Right-click in the editor pane and select Save.**

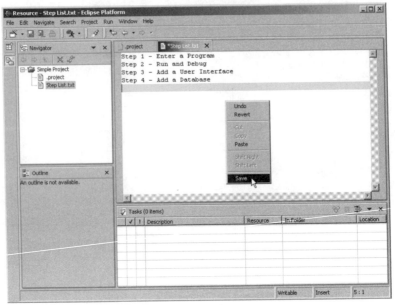

Figure 4.18: Save the contents of the file with the popup menu.

Congratulations! You have successfully created your own text file. You could now export that to some other directory, or go on to do something else.

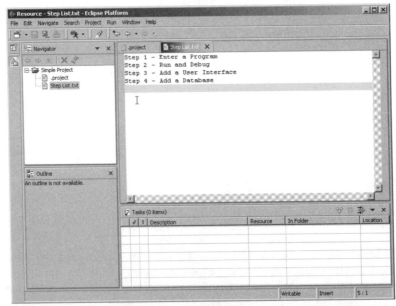

Figure 4.19: The updated workbench, with the Navigator view showing the new file.

Step 4.4—Create a folder, move your file into the folder

GOAL

In this step, you will create a folder
and move your newly created file into the folder.

While your project is hardly cluttered at this point (having only two files), I'm sure you can see how a flat project structure will eventually get filled up with files. However, Eclipse is up to the task, allowing you to create folders and move resources between them quite easily.

❑ **4.4(a) Right-click in the Navigator pane and select New/Folder . . .**

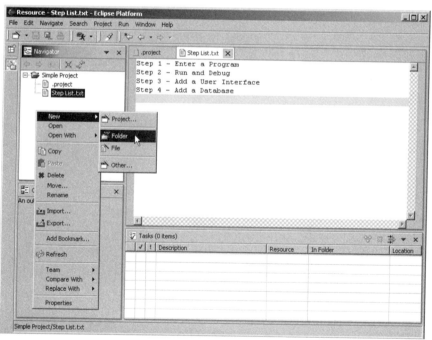

Figure 4.20: Right-clicking anywhere in the Navigator pane allows you to select the New submenu. Then select the Folder . . . option to bring up the wizard.

It should be no surprise that this brings up a wizard.

❑ **4.4(b) Enter 'Steps' in the Folder name field and click Finish.**

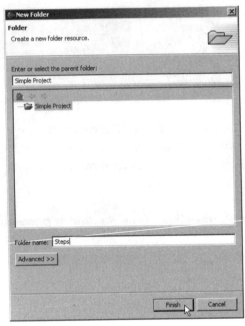

Figure 4.21: The New Folder wizard.

You'll see that the Steps folder has been added to your project, as shown in Figure 4.22. Moving the file Step List.txt to the Steps folder is a standard Windows-style drag and drop operation.

❏ **4.4(c) Left-click on the Step List.txt file and hold the mouse button down.**

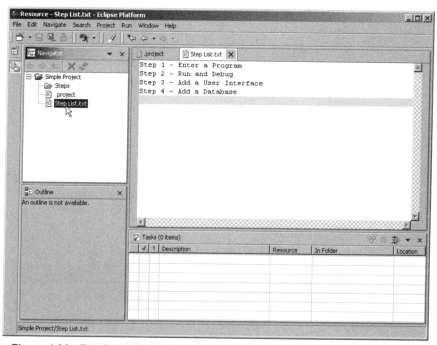

Figure 4.22: The Steps folder has been created.

❏ **4.4(d) Drag the Step List.txt file to the Steps folder and drop it.**

Continue holding the mouse button down and move the pointer towards the Steps folder. You'll see the cursor icon change to a pointer dragging a box. This is the standard *drag* icon, and indicates that you are dragging the selected item (Step List.txt, which now has a box around it). You *drop* the file into the folder by moving the pointer onto the folder—you'll know you've gotten there because the folder is selected—and then letting go of the mouse button.

There is also a Move. . . option in the popup menu for a resource that will accomplish the same thing without so much of a need for manual dexterity.

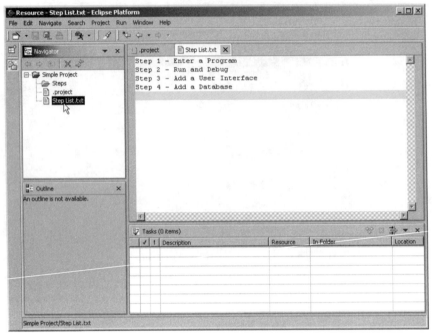

Figure 4.23: Dragging the Steps List.txt file and dropping it into the Steps folder.

You'll see that the Steps folder now has something in it, as indicated by the plus sign to its left.

❏ 4.4(e) Expand the Steps folder.

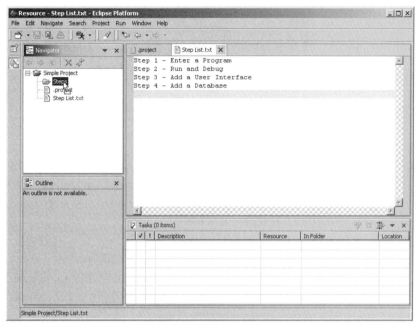

Figure 4.24: The Steps folder is no longer empty.

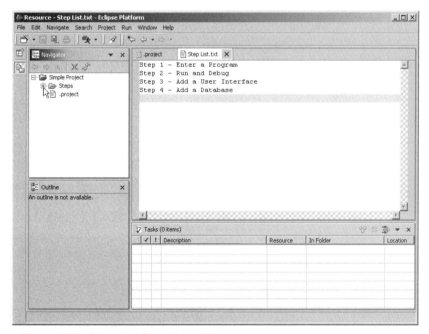

Figure 4.25: It has the Step List.txt file in it!

Step 4.5—Side-by-side editing

> ### GOAL
>
> In this step, you will learn how to use
> the docking feature of Eclipse to place two
> editor panels side by side and then restack them.

One of the more powerful but less intuitive features of the Eclipse IDE is something they call "docking". I think of it as "split screen" or "tiling" or "side by side," where I can take two stacked panels and place them side by side so that I can see both. If I want, I can then restack the panels.

Eclipse does this quite well via the docking concept, but it takes a little bit of getting used to. Basically, it's all done through a drag-and-drop mechanism. Dragging an editor tab to the border of the editor panel will change the cursor to a docking cursor and allow you to split the panel.

Dragging a tab from one split pane to another moves it. Moving the last tab out of a pane deletes the pane. You can split horizontally or vertically, and you can split the panes as many times as you wish, with the practical limit being the amount of screen real estate you have.

We're using an 800x600 screen in this manual for readability, so there isn't a lot of real estate, but in larger screen sizes this feature is very powerful, since you can easily cut and paste or drag and drop from one pane to another.

❑ **4.5(a) Select the Step List.txt editor tab and drag it downward.**

Remember, dragging is done by clicking on an object with the left mouse button, holding the button down, and moving the cursor with the mouse.

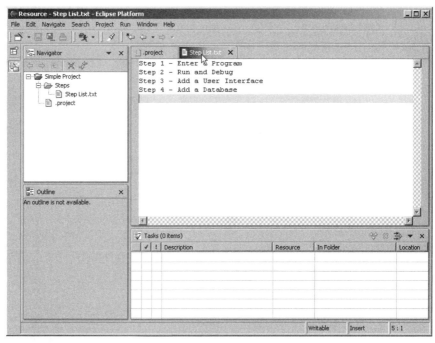

Figure 4.26: First, select the Step List.txt file, but hold down the cursor button.

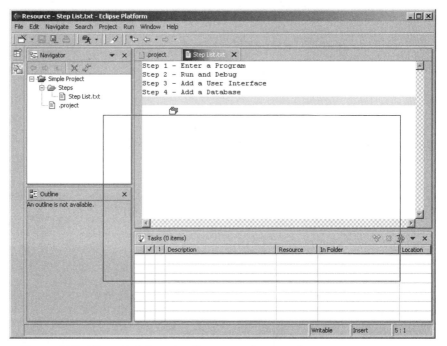

Figure 4.27: Then start dragging the cursor downward.

You'll notice that the cursor icon changes to a stack of folders. This indicates that you can drop this folder into this stack. This is not the docking cursor.

❑ **4.5(b) Drag the cursor to the left border of the editor panel.**

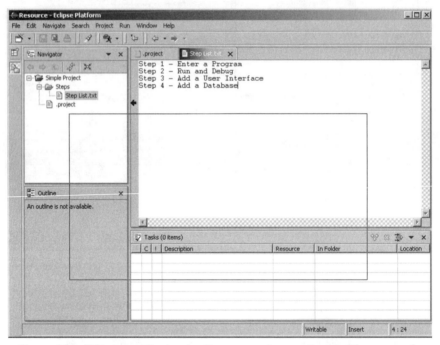

Figure 4.28: When you hit a border, the cursor changes to a docking cursor (a heavy arrow).

The cursor changes to a heavy left-pointing arrow. This is the docking cursor. It indicates that you can now drop the tab, and it will split the pane to the left.

❑ **4.5(c) Drop the editor (release the mouse button).**

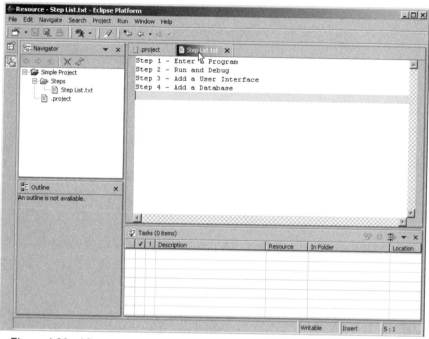

Figure 4.29: After successfully docking the Step List.txt editor, you now have a split panel.

This is the side-by-side or tiled effect we were trying to achieve. Not very intuitive, as I said, but very easy once you get the hang of it. I suggest playing with this a bit. By dragging the cursor to the top, right or bottom half of the panel, you can split in any of those directions. A split panel can be resplit as many times as is practical based on you display resolution.

Now that you can split panels, you need to know how to merge the split panels once again. That's not particularly intuitive either, but once you know the trick it's very simple.

❏ 4.5(d) Click and drag the .project tab.

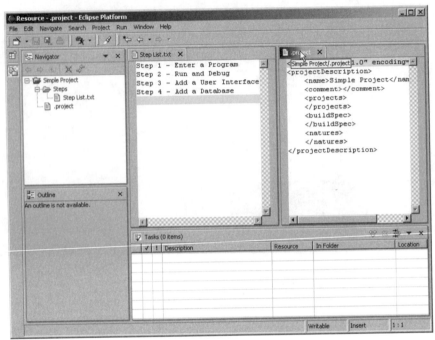

Figure 4.30: Getting ready to rejoin the panes: first, drag the .project editor.

❑ 4.5(e) Drop the .project tab on the Step List.txt pane.

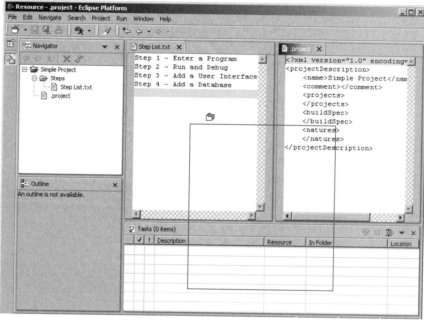

Figure 4.31: Drop the .project tab on the Step List.txt editor.

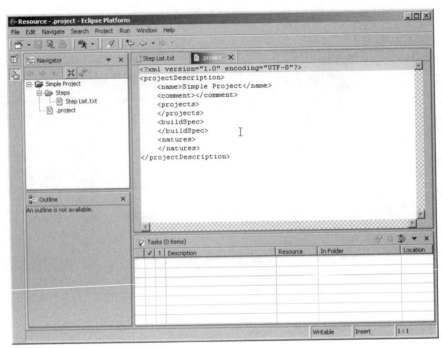

Figure 4.32: And they're together again!

This last drag-and-drop rejoined the .project editor with the Step List.txt editor. Since the stack that used to hold the .project editor is now empty, it is removed from the screen. By now, you should have a reasonable comfort level with using the editor, opening files, moving them around in your project and so on.

Next, it's time to look at a more specific perspective, namely the Java perspective.

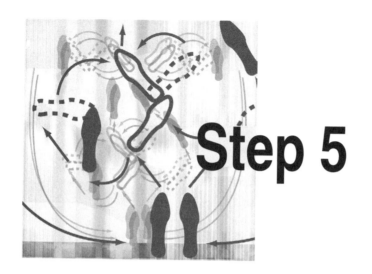

Step 5

The Java perspective

The Resource perspective you used in the last step is probably the one you are least likely to use on a regular basis. Because the Resource perspective assumes no knowledge about the contents of the various resources, that means it really can't help you that much, other than to organize things.

Now, if you were just gathering together various PC objects, such as pictures and text documents and the like, and then putting them in a ZIP file, then the Resource perspective might actually be of some help. But you can do pretty much the same thing with Windows Explorer, so the Resource perspective is in general not very useful. However, it *is* quite useful in one very specialized way, and I'll show you what that is a little later in this step.

However, the primary focus of this step is going to be using the Java perspective, and so let's get started on that.

Overview

The Eclipse SDK ships with three different features: the Eclipse Platform, the Java Development Tooling (JDT), and the Plug-in Development Environment (PDE). The Eclipse Platform consists of little more than the base libraries and the Resource perspective, which you reviewed in the previous step, while the PDE requires a whole book by itself. What we *can* cover is the JDT.

The JDT includes several different components. The Java perspective is just one of three new perspectives added as part of the JDT; the others include the Java Browsing perspective and the Java Type Hierarchy perspective. We won't spend a lot of time in this book covering those last two, although those of you who are familiar with Visual Age for Java might recognize the Java Browsing perspective as being very similar to the Packages tab on the workbench.

Instead, throughout this book, and in this step in particular, you'll be spending most of your time in the Java perspective. There are many ways of opening a perspective, but in this step you're going to take advantage of the fact that creating a certain kind of project can trigger the switch to a corresponding perspective. In this case, you will create a Java project, and you will see how Eclipse automatically switches to the appropriate perspective, the Java perspective.

So, without further ado, let's create some Java.

Step 5.1—Clean up your workbench

GOAL

In this step, you will clean up some of the things lying around from the last step.

I'll show you a quick way to tidy up the Navigator pane. The rightmost button of the Navigator toolbar is a set of four arrows pointing inward. If you roll your mouse over the button, the tool tip will come up saying "Collapse All". As the tip implies, this button will collapse all of your expanded folders and projects.

❑ **5.1(a) Click the Collapse All button on the Navigator toolbar.**

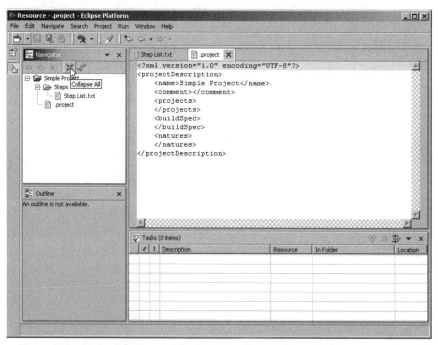

Figure 5.1: Clicking Collapse All collapses all projects and folders.

Okay, now that the projects are closed, I'd like you to close the documents you had open as well. This is done by rolling your cursor over the tab for each document in the editor pane and then clicking on the X that appears.

❏ 5.1(b) Close the Step List.txt resource.

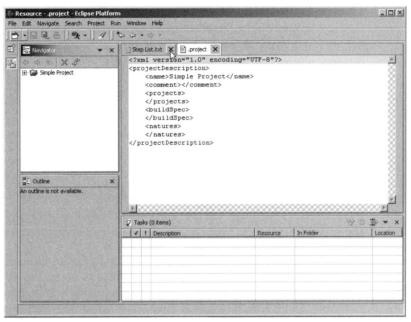

Figure 5.2: Close the Step List.txt document by clicking on the X.

❏ 5.1(c) Close the .project resource.

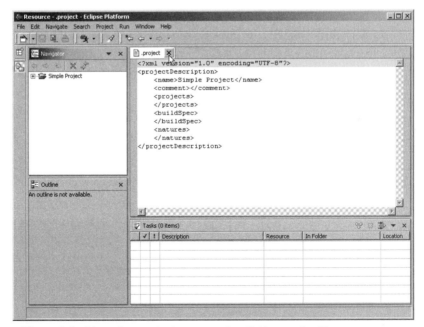

Figure 5.3: Close the .project resource by clicking on the X.

Step 5.2—Create a New Project

> ### GOAL
> You will create a new project.
> This will be a Java project. The IDE will
> automatically switch to the Java perspective.

As you add more plug-ins to your workbench, you will find that you have more and more options. For example, the base Eclipse Platform allows you to create projects only of a very simple type. The JDT and the PDE both add their own project types. The JDT adds the type Java Project.[1]

Note: This feature, like so many others, is configurable. Use the Windows/ Preferences option, then on the Workbench/Perspectives page check or uncheck "Switch to recommended perspective" under "New project options" to enable or disable this auto-switch feature.

Let's take the shortcut, shall we?

Okay, now you've got a nice clean workbench, so it's time to create a new project (and get things all messy again!). Remember that the right button of the mouse brings up context-sensitive popup menus.

---

[1] The PDE adds several other project types, but you don't have to worry about those in this book. When you create a new Java Project, Eclipse will automatically switch to the appropriate perspective, which happens to be the Java perspective, the one we'll be concentrating on in this book. So, you could either switch to the Java perspective yourself manually and then create a new Java Project, or follow the actions in this step to take a shortcut.

❑ 5.2(a) Right-click on the Navigator pane and select New/Project . . .

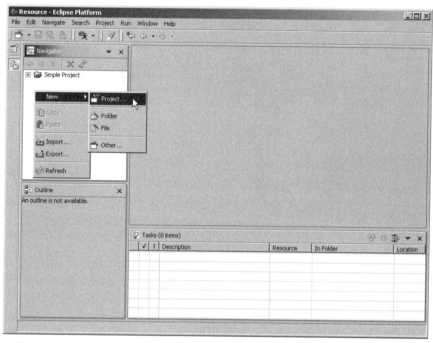

Figure 5.4: Bring up the New Project wizard by right-clicking on the Navigator.

Use the New Project wizard to select the type of project you are creating. For more complex projects, you may be asked for more information, but for a basic Java project, it's pretty simple.

❑ **5.2(b) Select Java on the left, select Java Project on the right, and click Next.**

Figure 5.5: Select Java and Java Project and click Next.

Enter the name and click Finish.

❑ **5.2(c) Type in 'Hello' and click Finish.**

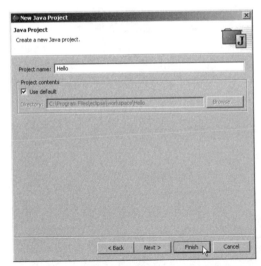

Figure 5.6: Finish the wizard by entering the name and clicking Finish.

A prompt will come up, asking you if you want to switch perspectives. Click the "Don't show me this message again" box and then click Yes.

❏ **5.2(d) Check 'Do not show this message again' and click Yes.**

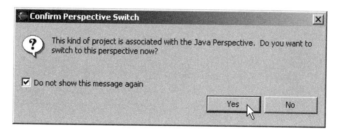

Figure 5.7: Make sure "Do not show this message again" is checked, then click Yes.

You should notice a couple of things. First, a new Hello project is shown in the left-hand pane. If you examine the title bar, you'll see that you're no longer in the Resource perspective but have been switched to the Java perspective. Notice also that the Outline pane has moved from the lower left of the workbench to the upper right. Finally, you'll see that a new icon has appeared in the perspective bar on the left of the workbench, and that new icon (the Java perspective icon) is selected.

Now, take a look at the contents of the newly created Hello project.

❑ 5.2(e) Expand the Hello project.

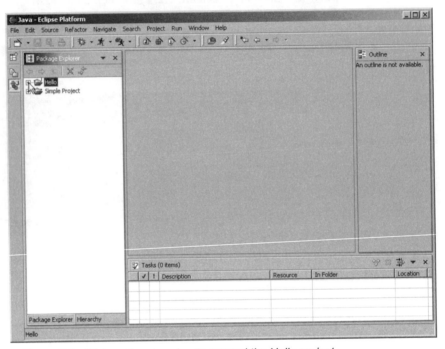

Figure 5.8: Click on the plus sign to expand the Hello project.

You'll see that the project doesn't contain much. However, it isn't quite empty, either. This is how Eclipse plug-ins work; they can preload your projects with things that are needed. If you decide to build your own plug-ins, you'll be able to do the same thing, and customize the projects specifically to your environment. In the case of the JDT plug-in, a new Java Project is preloaded with a classpath containing the current Java runtime JAR file.

It's difficult to see the full name of the JAR file because of the size of the pane and the length of the path to the JVM.

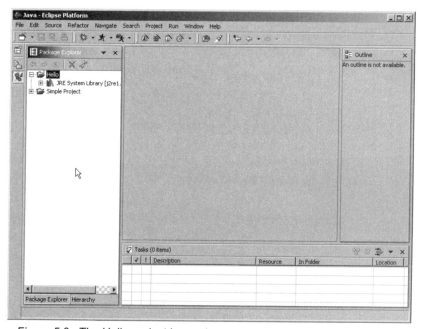

Figure 5.9: The Hello project is nearly empty, but not quite: A JAR file has been added by default.

❑ **5.2(f) Roll your cursor over the runtime JAR file.**

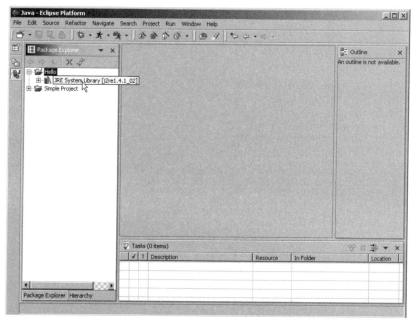

Figure 5.10: Rolling your mouse pointer over the JAR file shows its full name in a tool tip.

When you roll your cursor over the JAR file, the full file name shows up in a tool tip. This JAR file was selected when you installed Eclipse. As with so many other things in Eclipse, you can change this default by going into the Preferences (use the Window/Preferences option from the main menubar). For this course, the default is fine.

Before going on, collapse the project again. It's a little exercise, and it makes the display a little less cluttered.

❏ **5.2(g) Collapse the project.**

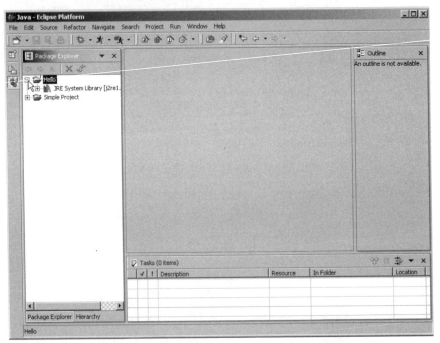

Figure 5.11: Click on the minus sign to collapse the Hello project.

Step 5.3—Look under the hood with the Resource perspective

GOAL

In this step, you will switch to the Resource perspective and review your newly created project.

I've already mentioned that the Resource perspective has no "specialized" knowledge of the various projects and resources, such as by more sophisticated plug-ins might provide. Because of this very limitation, however, the Resource perspective can be used to get a different view of things—sort of an "under the hood" look. You don't need to know how to do this for day-to-day operations, so this step is purely optional. If you're not interested in how the IDE works internally, you may want to skip ahead to Step 5.3. Otherwise, let me show you a few cool things about Eclipse.

First, switch back to the Resource perspective.

❑ **5.3(a) Click on the Resource perspective icon in the perspective bar.**

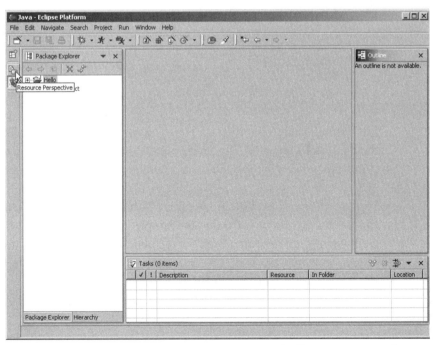

Figure 5.12: Use the perspective bar to change to the Resource perspective.

You'll notice that the Hello project has been collapsed. I want you to expand the Hello project. But before you do, I'd like you to try and predict what you're going to find in the project. You might want to flip back to Steps 4.2(g) and 4.2(h).

❑ 5.3(b) Expand the Hello project.

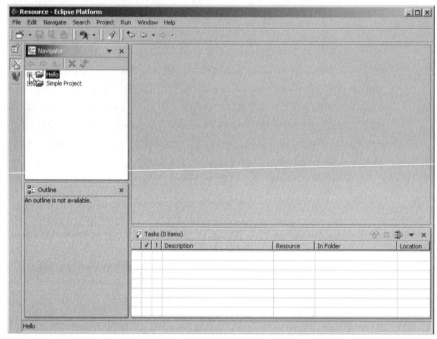

Figure 5.13: Left-click on the plus sign to expand the Hello project.

Interesting! There's a .project file, as you might have guessed after looking back at Step 4.2, as I suggested. However, I would have thought that we would see a JAR file in the project, but instead there's another document, called .classpath.

Well, we'll leave that little riddle alone for now; instead, we'll compare the .project file for this project with the one for Simple Project. To compare the two files, I'll walk you through opening each one up and then viewing them side by side.

First, open the .project file in Hello by double-clicking on it.

❏ **5.3(c) Open the .project file in project Hello.**

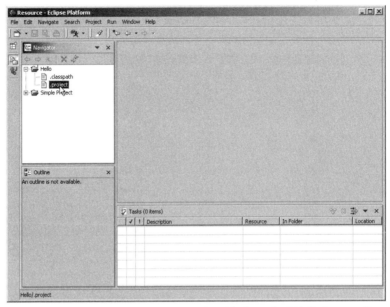

Figure 5.14: Double-click on the .project file in project Hello to open it.

The .project file will be opened up in the editor pane as shown in Figure 5.15.

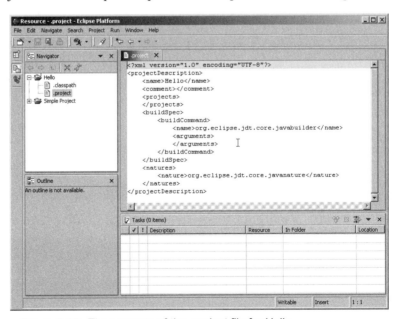

Figure 5.15: The contents of the .project file for Hello.

Next, expand Simple Project.

❑ 5.3(d) Expand Simple Project.

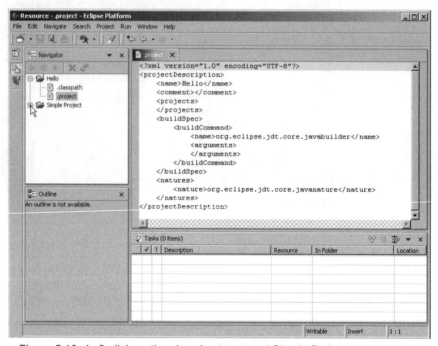

Figure 5.16: Left-click on the plus sign to expand Simple Project.

Open the .project file (remember, one way to open a file is to double-click on it).

❑ 5.3(e) Open the .project file for Simple Project.

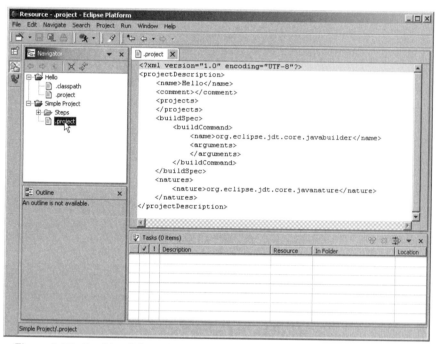

Figure 5.17: Double-click on the .project file in Simple Project.

Double-clicking the .project file will cause the .project file from Simple Project to open up in the same editor pane, overlaying the .project file from Hello. However, you can't see them side by side this way, so the next thing is to split the pane. This is done by docking (you may want to review Step 4.5 for a reminder of how docking works).

Click on the tab for .project of the Hello project, drag it down and to the left until the black arrow appears, and then drop it. This will dock the file and split the pane.

❏ **5.3(f) Drag the left file to the left border and drop it.**

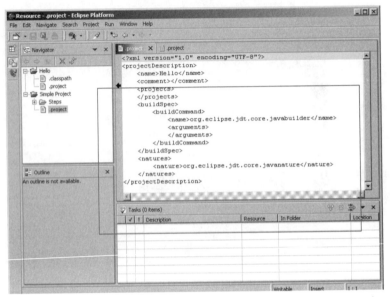

Figure 5.18: Dock Hello's .project file by dragging and dropping it on the left edge of the pane.

You'll see a display like the one in Figure 5.19.

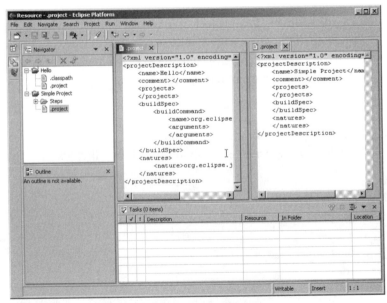

Figure 5.19: The two .project files side by side.

You might note that the Java project has a buildCommand entry in the buildSpec keyword as well as a nature entry in the natures keyword. What these particular values do is beyond the scope of this document, and in fact it's not easy to find even by looking through the Eclipse documentation. You'll need to do some research on your own to see how some of these things work.

Before we close up shop on this step, I'd like you to take a look at the other file generated for this project: the .classpath file.

First, close the .project file for Simple Project. Remember, you do this by rolling over the tab and then clicking on the X that appears. Since that's the only file in the right pane, the split will disappear.

❏ **5.3(g) Close the .project file for Simple Project.**

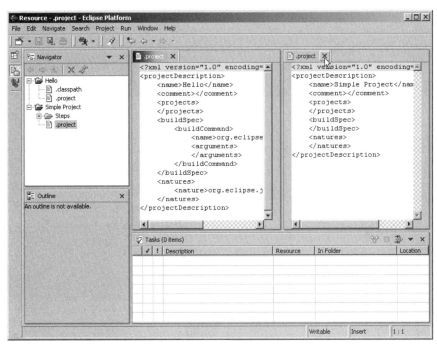

Figure 5.20: Close the .project file by clicking on the X.

❑ **5.3(h) Open the .classpath file.**

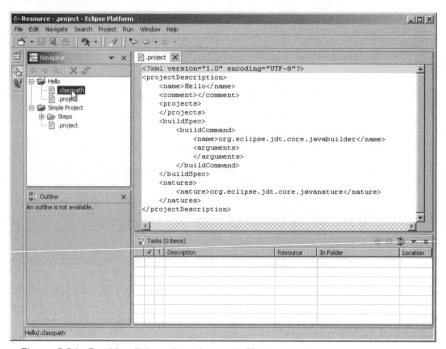

Figure 5.21: Double-click on the .classpath file to open it.

Since we're at a somewhat limited resolution, you can't actually see the contents of the file. This happens sometimes, and the easiest way around it is to maximize the view or editor by double-clicking on the appropriate tab.

In this case, double-click on the .classpath tab.

❏ **5.3(i) Maximize the .classpath pane.**

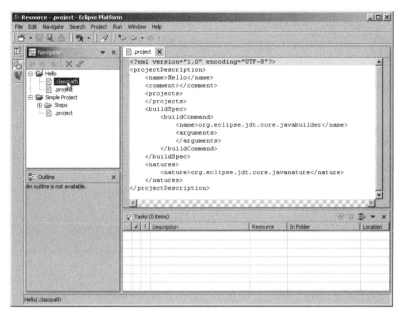

Figure 5.22: Double-click on the .classpath tab in the editor to maximize it.

What you'll see is a display like the one in Figure 5.23:

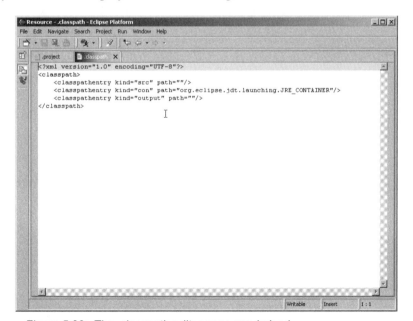

Figure 5.23: The .classpath editor pane maximized.

You'll note that there are actually several entries in this file. Not only can you see a couple of entries for "src" and "output", but there is also a "con" entry, which seems to define the runtime JAR file but has an odd syntax to it that looks like a cross between a package name and a substitution variable. While we don't have time to delve into this in detail, some experimenting on your part (perhaps with changing values when you add a Java project) may give you more insight.

I know this step hasn't provided a lot of detailed information; it wasn't meant to. What I wanted to do was to show you this technique so that you can at least see how to peek under the covers of Eclipse. There's nothing more frustrating than a black box that doesn't work. While this step won't explain everything, it will at least start you on the path of demystifying the IDE. Remember, it's not magic—it's just code.

Okay, play time is over. Let's clean up and move on.

Restore the editor pane for .classpath. This is the reverse of maximizing it—simply double-click on it again.

❑ **5.3(j)   Restore the .classpath.**

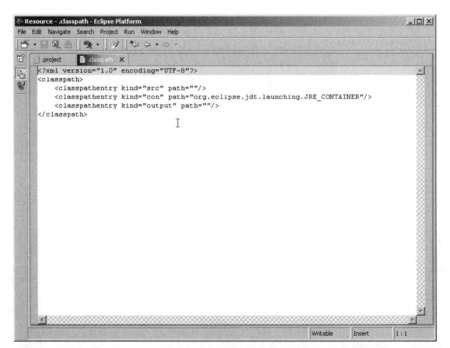

Figure 5.24: Restore the .classpath editor pane by double-clicking on it.

❑ **5.3(k) Close the .classpath editor pane.**

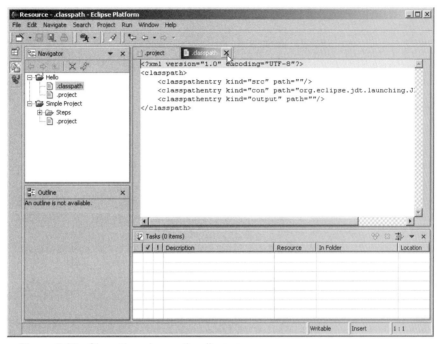

Figure 5.25: Close the .classpath editor pane.

□ **5.3(I) Close the .project editor pane.**

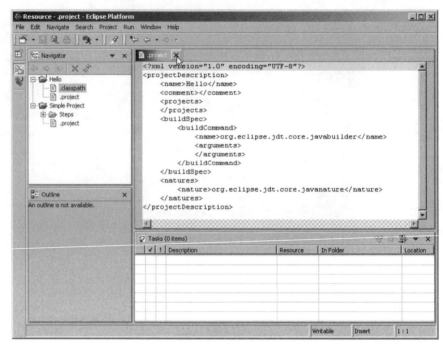

Figure 5.26: Close the .project editor pane.

Finally return to the Java perspective to get some work done. Switching perspectives is most easily accomplished by using the perspective bar on the left of the workbench.

❑ **5.3(m) Switch to the Java perspective.**

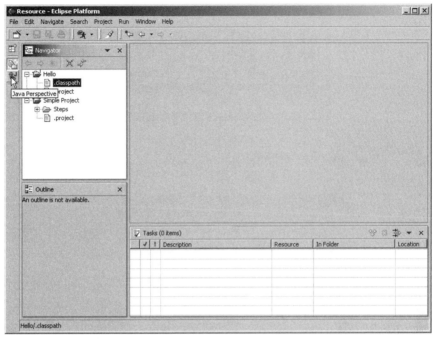

Figure 5.27: Switch to the Java perspective.

Step 5.4—Explore the Java perspective

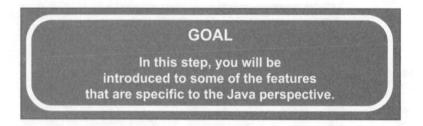

GOAL

In this step, you will be
introduced to some of the features
that are specific to the Java perspective.

Your workbench should currently look like the one in Figure 5.28.

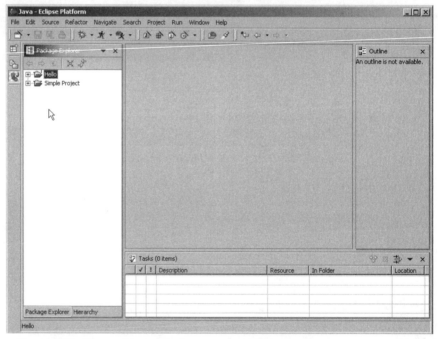

Figure 5.28: The workbench in Java perspective.

If you were to compare this view to the one of the basic Resource perspective (such as the one shown in Figure 3.5), you would notice several differences. First, there are some additional options in the main menu bar.

❑ 5.4(a) View the Source menu.

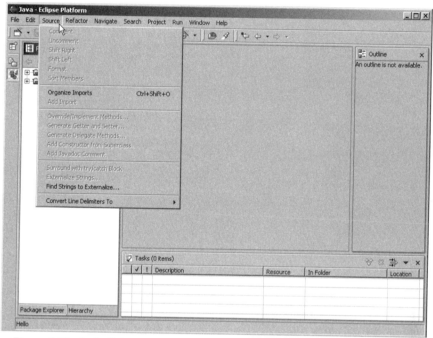

Figure 5.29: Left-click on the Source option on the menu bar to see the Source menu.

Most of the options are currently grayed out (disabled), because you don't have any resources selected, just a project. However, as you can see, there are quite a few options.

Similarly, you can view the Refactor menu, which also has a number of options.

❏ 5.4(b) View the Refactor menu.

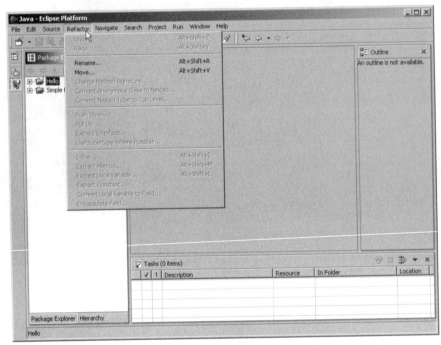

Figure 5.30: Left-click on the Refactor option to see the Refactor menu.

There are also several new options on the main tool bar.

❏ 5.4(c) Roll your cursor over the main tool bar to see Java-specific options.

As you roll your cursor over the main tool bar, tool tips appear, identifying each option, as shown in Figures 5.31 through 5.37.

Figure 5.31: The Debug tool.

Figure 5.32: The Run tool.

Figure 5.33: The New Java Project tool.

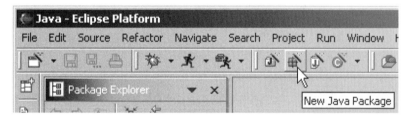

Figure 5.34: The New Java Package tool.

Figure 5.35: The New Scrapbook Page tool.

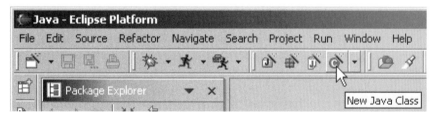

Figure 5.36: The New Java Class tool.

Figure 5.37: The Open Type tool.

The last new feature in the Java perspective is the Hierarchy view. There's nothing in it right now, but I'll at least show you how to get to it.

You'll see two tabs at the bottom of the left-hand pane: Package Explorer and Hierarchy. If you look closely, you'll see that the Package Explorer view is selected, but it's easier to tell by just looking at the title bar on the top of the pane.

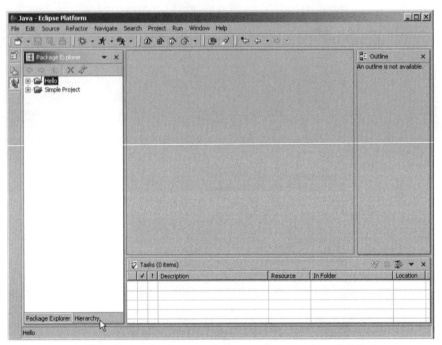

Figure 5.38: The tabs at the bottom of a pane allow you to switch between stacked views.

Switching to the Hierarchy view is simple: Just click on the word "Hierarchy" in the bottom tab list.

❏ **5.4(d) Click on the Hierarchy tab to switch to the Hierarchy view.**

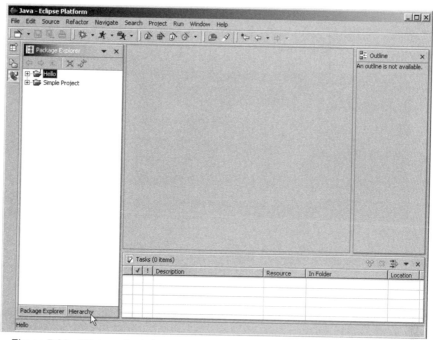

Figure 5.39: Click on the tab to switch to the corresponding view; in this case, the Hierarchy tab.

The hierarchy view is empty at this point. This is just an example of stacked views, similar to those in the editor pane. In fact, you can also "dock" the panels in a stacked view, creating multiple panes. We won't bother with that here, but that might be something you want to explore. If you find that you've made the perspective unusable, you can always restore the defaults using the menu option Window/Reset Perspective.

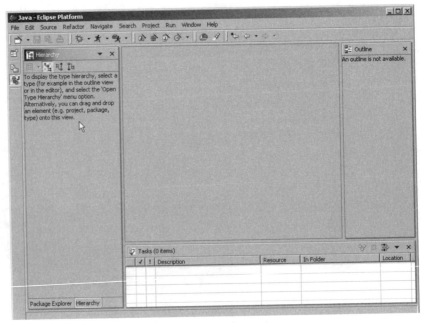

Figure 5.40: The Hierarchy view, currently empty.

❏ **5.4(e) Click on the Package Explorer tab to switch back.**

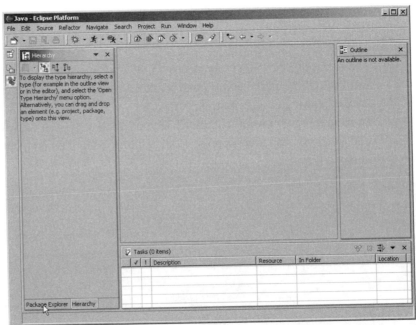

Figure 5.41: Click on the Package Explorer tab to return to the Package Explorer view.

You'll see a display like the one in Figure 5.42. You're ready to proceed to Step 6.

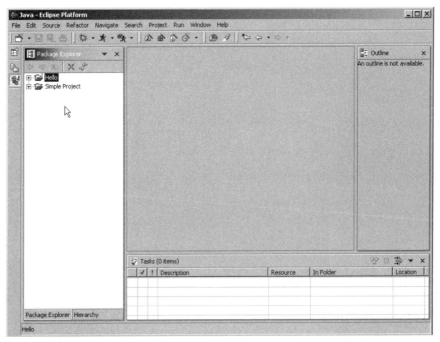

Figure 5.42: And here you are on the Package Explorer, ready for Step 6.

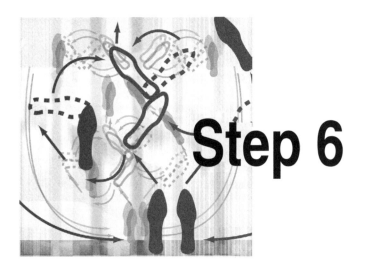

Step 6

The Debug perspective

So far you've seen the Resource perspective and the Java perspective. These two were similar to one another because they served a similar purpose: group sets of objects, and then allow navigation and manipulation of those objects. The major difference is that the Java perspective is a bit more focused and specific. Many perspectives will be of this nature; I call them navigation perspectives, or sometimes just navigators.

There are other kinds of perspectives, however. Some perspectives are geared toward a single task. The Debug perspective is one of those. It has special views and a layout specifically designed to allow you as the programmer to interact with the currently running program and perform the various activities associated with debugging, such as setting breakpoints and inspecting variables. In this step, I'll very briefly introduce you to the Debug perspective. The two of you will become much better acquainted in Part II.

✔ Here is your step checklist:

Step 6.1—Open the Debug perspective

GOAL

In this step, you will open the Debug
perspective using Eclipse's main menu bar.

This is another way to open a perspective. To get to the Java perspective, you opened
a new Java project. If that were the only way to switch to a new perspective, you'd
have a lot of junk projects, but of course that's not your only option. In this step,
you'll use the main menu bar to open and close the Debug perspective.

❑ **6.1(a) From the main menu bar, select the Window menu.**

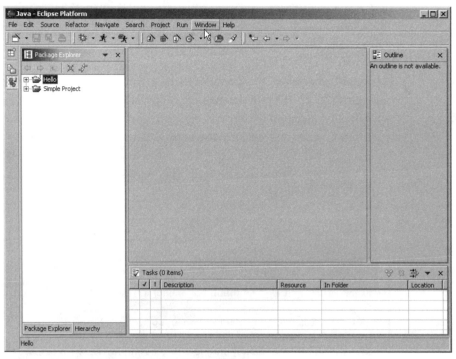

Figure 6.1: Select the Window option on the main menu bar.

❏ **6.1(b) Select Open Perspective/Debug.**

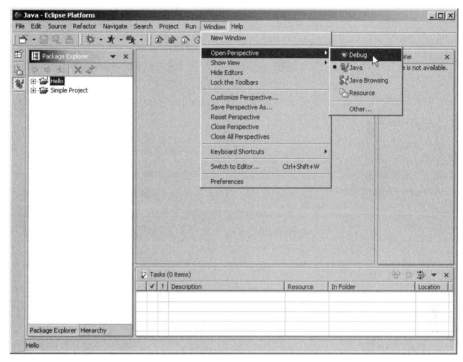

Figure 6.2: Select Open Perspective/Debug to switch to the debug perspective.

Figure 6.3 shows the Debug perspective. There's not much to see at this point, since you have no programs running, but I wanted you to see a perspective that is significantly different in initial appearance from the usual navigator-type perspectives you've seen up to now.

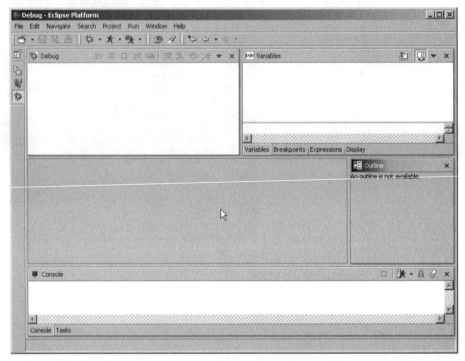

Figure 6.3: The Debug perspective, although it's pretty empty because nothing is running.

Note that a new icon (the little bug) has appeared on the perspective bar at the left. Whenever you open a new perspective, its icon shows up on the perspective bar. You can also switch perspectives and open and close them from the perspective bar, but I'll leave that for another time.

Although the Debug perspective isn't particularly useful yet, you can at least wander around it a little bit. For example, the upper left pane is the debug pane. That pane has a toolbar with a number of options. Most are grayed out (disabled), but you can still roll your mouse pointer over them to get a hint.

If you roll over the buttons as shown in Figures 6.4 and 6.5, you'll see the Resume tool and the Step with Filters/Step Debug tool, both of which will be familiar to programmers who have used IDEs before. If you don't recognize them, don't worry; I'll explain them in detail in Part II.

Figure 6.4: The Resume tool button.

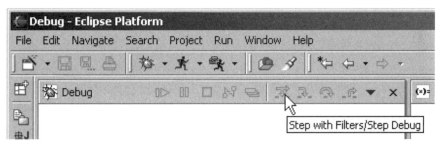

Figure 6.5: The Step with Filters tool button.

There are multiple ways to close a perspective, but the most straightforward is probably to use the main menu bar. Selecting Window/Close Perspective will close the currently displayed perspective.

❏ **6.1(c) From the main menu bar, select Window/Close Perspective.**

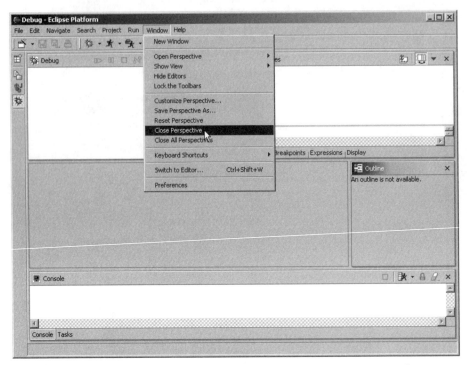

Figure 6.6: Select Window/Close Perspective to close the current perspective.

Closing this perspective will return you to the previous perspective, in this case the Java perspective. Note that the Debug perspective icon is no longer on the perspective bar.

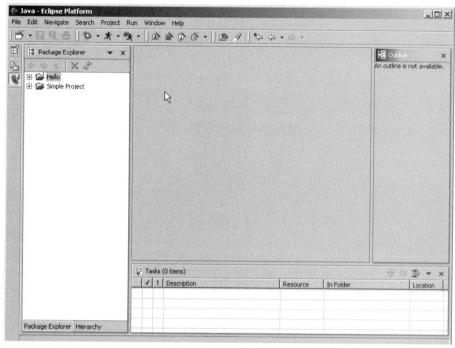

Figure 6.7: And now you're back to the Java perspective.

Now that you've seen most of the pieces of the Eclipse workbench as they relate to simple Java development, I think it's time that to begin a real project.

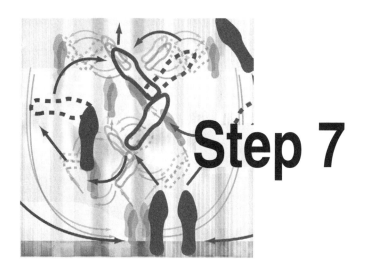

Step 7

A simple program

The book up to now has primarily been a familiarization with the Eclipse workbench. You didn't really create anything usable. However, now you're going to create a program that can actually display data from a database.

Not all at once, though! Instead, we'll proceed slowly. First, you'll create a very simple program, and then you'll debug it. After that you'll add a user interface and finally a database. This step will cover only that first task: creating the initial simple program.

Step 7.1—Get into the Java perspective

GOAL

In this step, you will open the Java
perspective using Eclipse's main menu bar.

If you're already in the Java perspective, you can skip this step and continue with
Step 7.2.

Note: The Title Bar of the Eclipse IDE will indicate which perspective you're
currently in. If your Title Bar says "Java - Eclipse Platform" as in Figure 7.1, then
you're ready to move on.

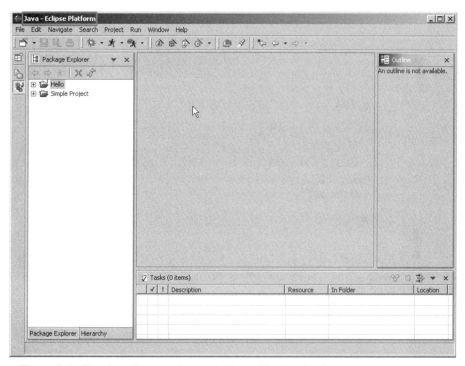

Figure 7.1: The Java Perspective, as indicated by the title bar.

Okay, for whatever reason, you're not in the Java perspective. Maybe you've skipped the first part of the book, or you were exploring, or whatever. You might be in the Resource explorer, as shown in Figure 7.2.

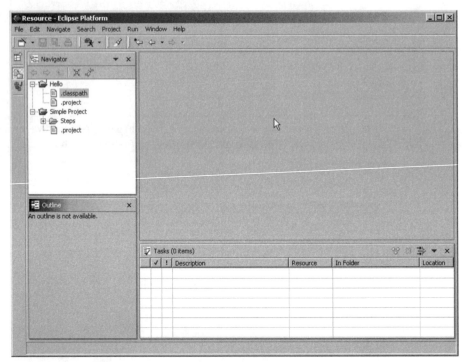

Figure 7.2: A possible alternative view of the IDE; in this case, the Resource perspective.

No matter where you are, our job now is to make sure you get to the proper perspective. That's actually quite easy. You can get to the Java perspective by using Eclipse's main menu bar.

❑ **7.1(a) From Eclipse's main menu bar, select Window/Open Perspective/ Java.**

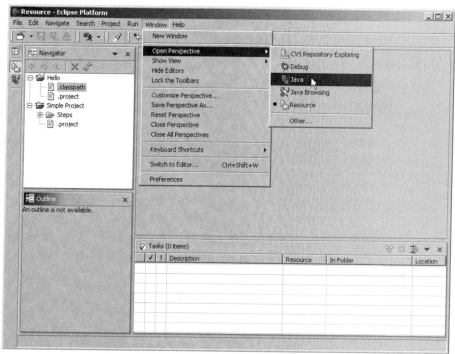

Figure 7.3: *Select Window/Open Perspective/Java from the main menu bar.*

The Java perspective will appear.

Step 7.2—Create the Java project

> ### GOAL
>
> In this step, you
> will create a Java project.

If you already see a project named Hello in your Package Explorer, as in Figure 7.4, then you may skip ahead to Step 7.3.

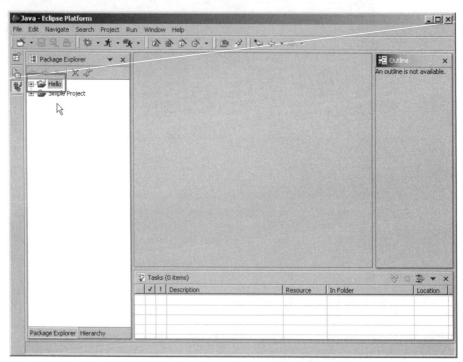

Figure 7.4: The Java perspective showing the Hello project.

Otherwise, you'll need to create a project. To do this, you'll simply do the same actions as outlined in Step 5.2.

❑ **7.2(a) Right-click on the Navigator pane and select New/Project . . .**

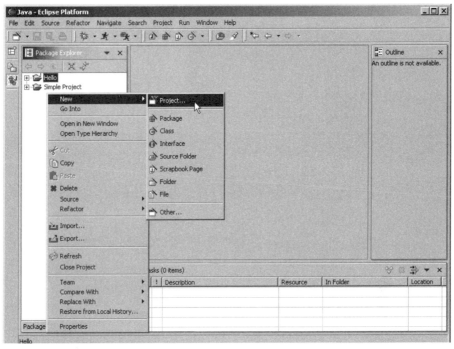

Figure 7.5: Bringing up the New Project wizard by right-clicking on the Navigator pane and selecting New/Project . . .

The New Project wizard will appear. Use it to select the type of project you are creating. For more complex projects, you may be asked for more information, but for a basic Java project, it's pretty simple.

❑ **7.2(b) Select Java on the left, Java Project on the right, and click Next.**

*Figure 7.6: Select Java and Java Project
on the left and right, and click Next.*

Enter the name, click Finish, and you're done.

❑ **7.2(c) Type in "Hello" and click Finish.**

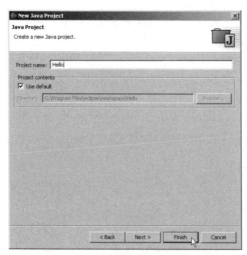

*Figure 7.7: Finish the wizard by entering
the name and clicking Finish.*

Step 7.3—Creating a new class

> ### GOAL
>
> **In this step, you will create a new Java class that you can actually run and debug (although debugging will wait for Step 8).**

Creating a class is quite easy, but how you do it depends on what you plan to do with the class. For this step, you'll be creating a class that you can actually run from the command line (or the console, as it's called within Eclipse).

❑ **7.3(a) Right-click on Hello in the Package Explorer and select New Class.**

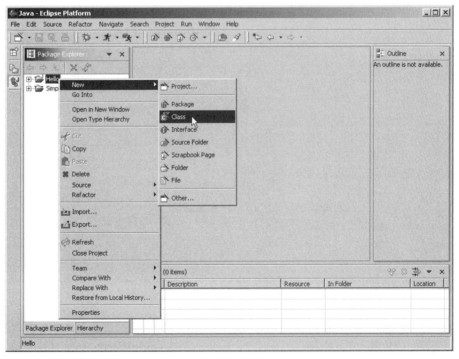

Figure 7.8: Creating a new class using New/Class.

❏ **7.3(b) Make sure the Source Folder is Hello.**

❏ **7.3(c) Leave Package blank.**

❏ **7.3(d) Leave Enclosing type unchecked.**

❏ **7.3(e) Enter HelloWorld in the Name field.**

❏ **7.3(f) Make sure public is checked, abstract and final are unchecked.**

❏ **7.3(g) Leave Superclass as java.lang.Object, Interfaces blank.**

❏ **7.3(h) Make sure public static void main(String[] args) is checked.**

❏ **7.3(i) Leave the other two unchecked.**

❏ **7.3(j) Click Finish.**

Figure 7.9: Setting the fields properly for a new class.

Following these steps will create a class HelloWorld in the default package (because you left Package blank) in project Hello. It will be a public class, neither abstract nor final. The class has no superclass (except for the implied superclass Object) and implements no interfaces. Finally, the IDE has been instructed to create a standard "main" method, but no other methods. That being the case, we will see the result as in Figure 7.10.

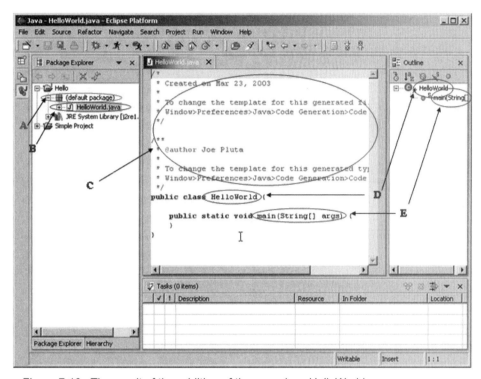

Figure 7.10: The result of the addition of the new class HelloWorld.

There are a number of interesting results from this simple operation.

A. A default package is added, with the icon. The default package is added because you left the package name blank in Step 7.3(c). Had you entered a package name, that package would have been created instead. Had you used an already existing package, the class would simply have been added to that package.

B. The class HelloWorld was added. More correctly, the Java source code was added. That's what the icon in the Package Explorer indicates. The class is also created; we'll look into this a little further in a moment.

C. A class is added with some initial comments. These comments are pretty useless at this point, but you can change them.

Note: To change the default documentation for a new class, go into Window/ Preferences. In the Preferences dialog, select Java/Templates and then edit the template named typecomment. You can modify quite a number of templates using this dialog.

D. The class itself is defined as HelloWorld. You'll also notice that the class is shown in the Outline view.

E. Last but not least, the main() method is created. It, too, has an entry in the Outline view.

Step 7.4—Write the code for the new class

> ## GOAL
>
> The last editing activity is to
> enter the code for this class. Up to this point,
> you've simply been defining a few basic attributes
> of your class, but now it' s time to write the code.

You may either enter the code directly into the editor or use the Import feature to import the source from the supplied CD-ROM. If you wish to enter the source yourself and get a feel for the source editor, use Option 1 below. Otherwise, skip ahead to Option 2.

Option 1—Source Entry

❑ **7.4(a) Enter the following source code as your main() method.**

```
System.out.println("Hello World!");
System.exit(0);
```

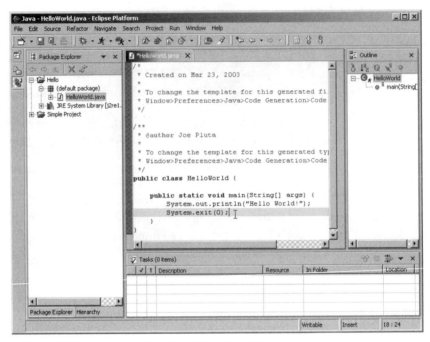

Figure 7.11: Source code entered into the editor pane.

❏ **7.4(b) Right-click in the editor pane and select Save.**

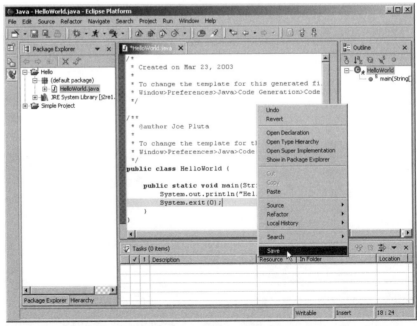

Figure 7.12: Right-click in the editor pane and select Save to save the code.

Another option is just to press Ctrl-S. At this point, you can skip ahead to Step 7.5. However, you might want to execute Option 2 anyway. This will import the code from the CD-ROM and overwrite the code you just entered. It will look exactly the same as what you typed in except for the author name, and you'll learn how to use the Import feature, which I'm sure you'll be using in the future.

Option 2—Importing Source from CD

Importing is quite easy. The only part that can get a little confusing is the relationship between folders and packages. When you are importing from a file system, you must be certain to import from the correct point in the file tree. To make it easy for this book, I have located the source for each step in a folder named for that step, as you are about to see.

❑ **7.4(c) Insert the included CD-ROM into your CD-ROM drive.**

❑ **7.4(d) Right-click on the Hello project and select Import . . .**

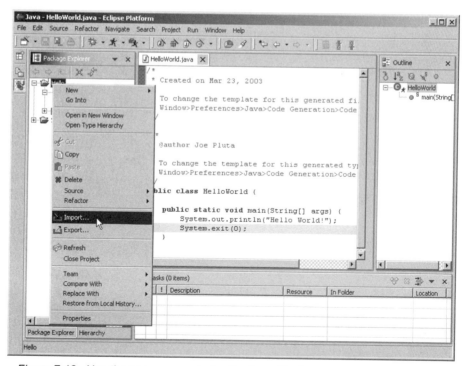

Figure 7.13: Use the popup menu in the Package Explorer to import a file into the Hello project.

The Import wizard gives you several options for your import source. Since your source is in a folder on the CD-ROM, you'll use the File system option.

❑ **7.4(e) Select File system in the Import wizard and click Next.**

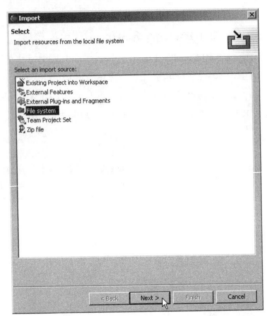

Figure 7.14: Select File system as the source for the import.

Now you need to specify the location of the files. All source for this step is located on the CD-ROM in a folder called Source, in a subfolder called Step 7, so specify

R:\Source\Step 7, where R is the letter of the CD-ROM drive where you loaded the disk. In Figure 7.15, the disk is loaded in the D: drive.

❑ **7.4(f) Enter "R:\Source\Step 7" in the From directory field, where R is the drive letter of your CD-ROM drive, and press the Tab key.**

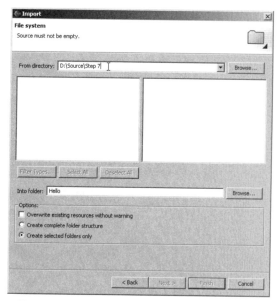

Figure 7.15: Enter R:\Source\Step 7, where R is the drive where you loaded the included CD-ROM.

The Tab key will cause the left pane to display an icon for the Step 7 folder. Select the Step 7 folder by clicking on it.

❑ **7.4(g) Left-click on the Step 7 folder.**

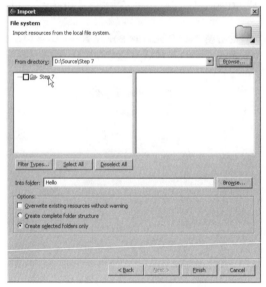

Figure 7.16: Select the Step 7 folder by left-clicking on it.

This will cause the contents of the Step 7 folder to appear in the right-hand pane as shown in Figure 7.17.

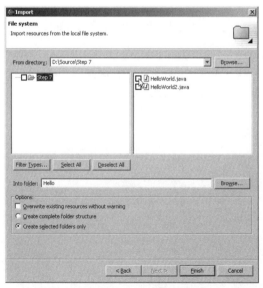

Figure 7.17: The contents of the Step 7 folder will appear in the right hand pane.

Select HelloWorld.java by clicking on its checkbox.

❑ **7.4(h) Select HelloWorld.java and click Finish.**

Figure 7.18: Select only HelloWorld.java, then click Finish.

If you also performed Option 1, you will get a confirmation dialog like the one in Figure 7.19.

❑ **7.4(i) Click Yes on the confirmation box that pops up.**

Figure 7.19: This prompt is used to be sure you really want to overwrite your source.

When you are done, your display should look just like the one shown in Figure 7.20. Since the source on the CD doesn't have all the fancy auto-generated comments, it'll be a little more austere than what the tool generated, as you can see.

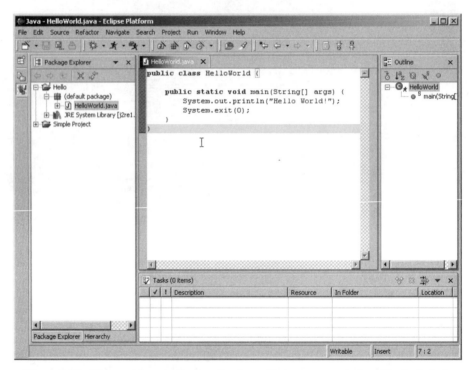

Figure 7.20: The workbench display after importing source code from the included CD-ROM.

Step 7.5—Reviewing the source and the generated class

GOAL

In this step, you will use the Package Explorer to verify that Eclipse automatically compiles code when you save it, and to inspect the generated class.

You may have noticed that when you added HelloWorld.java that it was expandable—you could see the little plus sign to the left, which indicated there were objects underneath it. That may seem a little unusual, since this is just a source file. In the Resource perspective you wouldn't see the plus sign. So why does the Java perspective see Java source files differently?

Well, it's because the Java perspective considers the Java source file to be the parent of the Java class file. Let's take a look. Expand the source by left-clicking on the plus sign as shown in Figure 7.21, which will in turn give you the display in Figure 7.22.

❏ **7.5(a) Expand HelloWorld.java.**

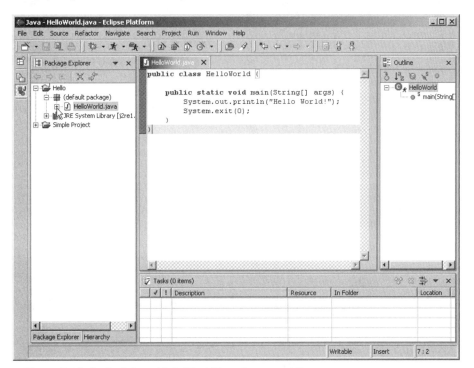

Figure 7.21: Left-click on HelloWorld.java to expand it.

You'll see that underneath HelloWorld.java source code, with the J icon, is the HelloWorld class, with a class icon. The white C inside a green circle denotes a class, and the little running guy underneath indicates that the class has a main() method and is therefore executable (i.e., runnable—cute, eh?).

You'll notice that the HelloWorld class, which is a child of the HelloWorld.java source code in the Package Explorer view, itself has a child. Each method in the class is considered a child of the class. So beneath the HelloWorld class, you see the main() method, with a green ball icon. The green ball indicates a public method, and the red S declares it to be static (Eclipse is big on icons declaring a lot of information).

Note also that these same symbols are used in the Outline view in the upper right-hand pane.

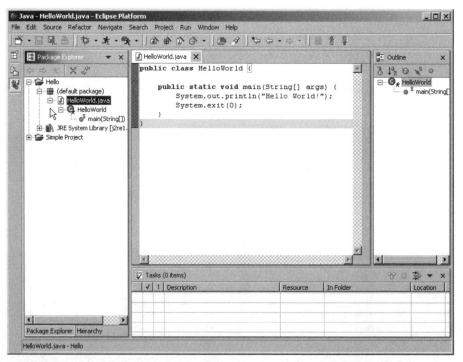

Figure 7.22: The expanded HelloWorld shows the source, the class, and the method.

Okay, you've entered the class. Now you get to run it. Step 8, here we come!

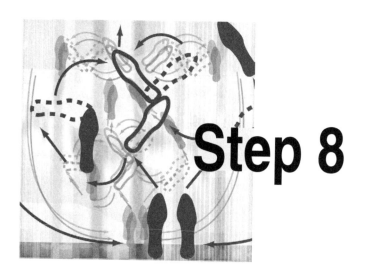

Step 8

Running and debugging

Are you ready to see the fruits of your labor? Ready for the payback for all that hard work? Well wait no more; it's time to start running things!

In this step, you'll run your program. Not only that, you'll set a breakpoint, start the program in debug mode, stop at the breakpoint, inspect and change a variable, and continue execution—all the steps needed to debug your programs.

✔ **Here is your step checklist:**

Step 8.1—Running your HelloWorld program

GOAL

In this step, you will run
the program you entered in Step 7.

Note: Some toolbar buttons, such as the Run button, also have a small dropdown symbol to the right. This dropdown brings up a secondary menu of options. The primary button usually will rerun the most recently selected option.

☐ **8.1(a) Select HelloWorld.java if it is not already selected.**

☐ **8.1(b) From the main tool bar, select the Run tool's dropdown.**

☐ **8.1(c) Select Run . . .**

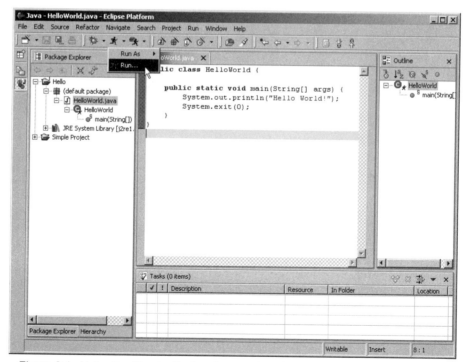

Figure 8.1: Using the Run tool's dropdown, select the Run . . option.

This brings up the "launch configuration" screen. There are several options here, but we will concentrate on the Java Application option. I hope to write an entire book someday on working with JUnit, but that's another issue for another day.

❑ **8.1(d) Select Java Application and click New.**

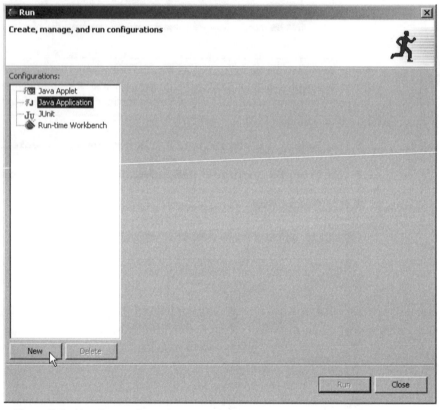

Figure 8.2: Use the configuration wizard to create a new Java Application configuration.

The next page of the wizard will come up. This is a very complicated page, because you can set all kinds of things. Note that several defaults are already set, such as the Project name (Hello) and the Main class to run (HelloWorld). As long as you don't need to pass parameters or set runtime JVM characteristics, these defaults are often good enough.

Note: There are times when you need to set certain runtime characteristics. We will see this when we use the SWT (Standard Widget Toolkit) classes in Step 9. But for these first examples, and in fact for many programming situations, the defaults are acceptable.

❑ **8.1(e) Leave the defaults as they are and press Run.**

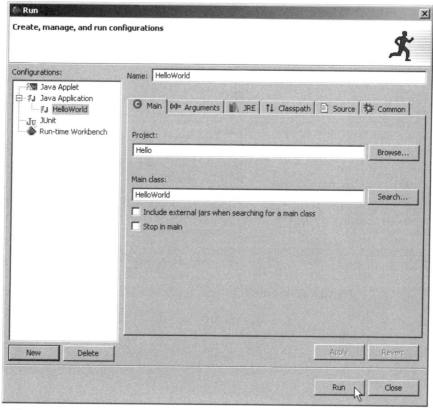

Figure 8.3: Leave the defaults (Project = Hello and Main class = HelloWorld) and press Run.

And here are your results! Since this very simple program does nothing more than print to the standard output, the results show up in the console window. The console window magically pops up on top of the Tasks view, and shows you the results of your programming.

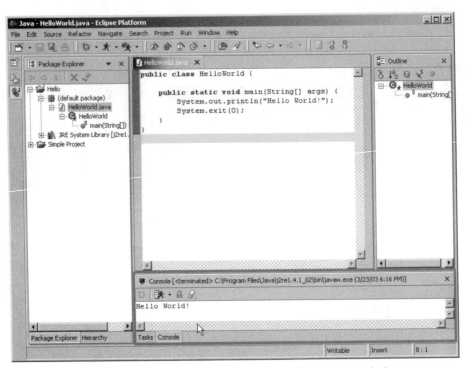

Figure 8.4: The results of your application show up in the console window.

Step 8.2—Create HelloWorld2

> ### GOAL
>
> In this step, you will copy the HelloWorld program to HelloWorld2 and make a minor modification that will allow you to do some debugging.

The original HelloWorld program doesn't do much; it just prints a literal string. That doesn't leave a lot of room for debugging. In this next program, you'll initialize a counter that you'll use to control a loop. Your goal will be to run it without debugging, then later, using the debugger, go in and modify the counter to make the program run differently. But first, you need to copy the program. Once again, I'll provide two options: source entry and import. And once again, I suggest you do both, just for practice. But if you're in a huge hurry, skip to Option 2.

Option 1—Source Entry

☐ **8.2(a) Right-click on HelloWorld.java and select Copy.**

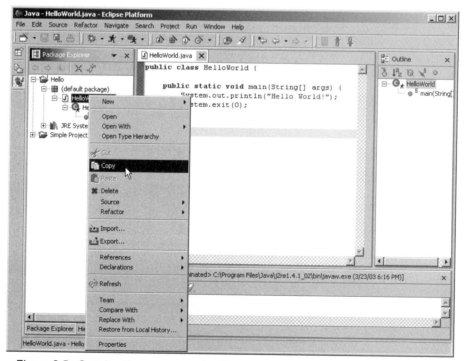

Figure 8.5: Copying the program using the popup menu.

❑ **8.2(b) Right-click on your default package and select Paste.**

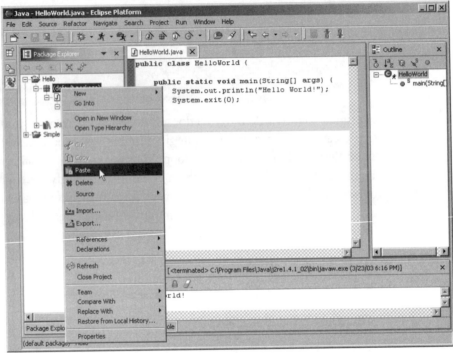

Figure 8.6: Getting ready to paste the source back into the default package.

This causes a name conflict, because HelloWorld already exists, so you have to address that in the Name Conflict window:

❑ **8.2(c) Enter 'HelloWorld2' and click OK.**

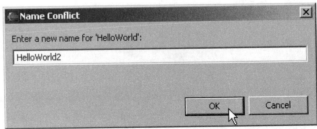

Figure 8.7: Change the name to resolve the conflict.

And that's all it takes to copy a source file!

Caution!!! Copying a file does not automatically open it! In Figure 8.8, you will see that the new file, HelloWorld2.java, is not open. Only the old file, HelloWorld.java, is open. I have on occasion forgotten this and modified the old program without realizing it! After copying a file, you must open it to edit it. The next steps will open the file.

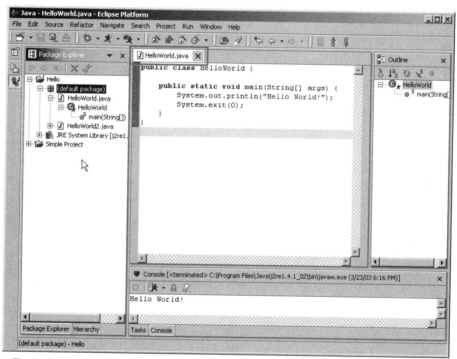

Figure 8.8: After copying the file, the old file is open, but the new file is not.

Use the popup menu to open the new file (right-click on the file to bring up the popup menu). You can also double-click on a file to use the default editor.

❑ **8.2(d) Right-click on HelloWorld2.java and select Open.**

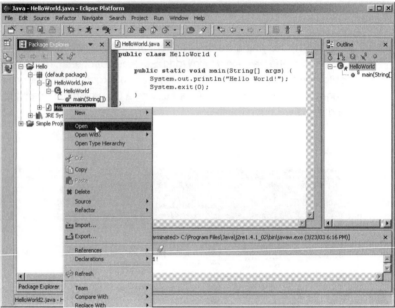

Figure 8.9: To open the new file, simply right-click on it and select Open (or double-click the file).

Now the new file is open.

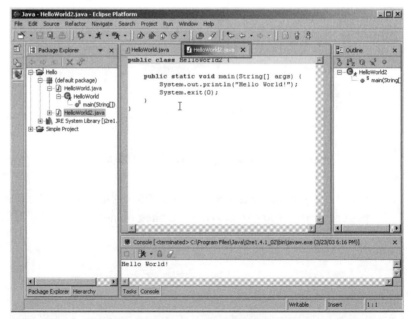

Figure 8.10: HelloWorld2 is now open in the editor, along with HelloWorld.

❑ **8.2(e) Modify the main method with the following source.**

```
int count = 3;
for (int i = 0; i < count; i++)
{
System.out.println("Hello" + i);
}
System.exit(0);
```

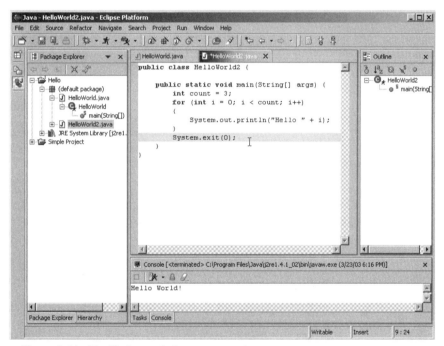

Figure 8.11: Modify the code to use a counter.

This code will use a counter (count) to loop three times, printing a slightly different message each time.

❑ **8.2(f) Right-click in the editor and select Save.**

You can also press Ctrl-S to save the source.

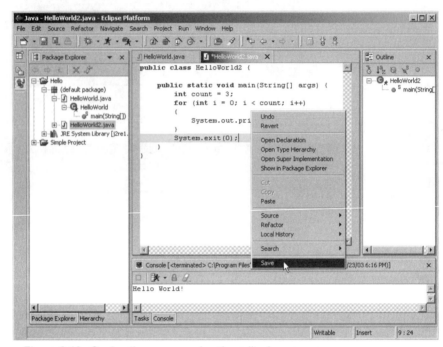

Figure 8.12: Saving the source using the editor's popup menu.

Option 2—Importing source from CD

If you've already performed Option 1, you can skip this section and go directly to Step 8.3. You could also execute this step; it won't hurt anything.

❑ **8.2(g) Right-click on the Hello project and select Import . . .**

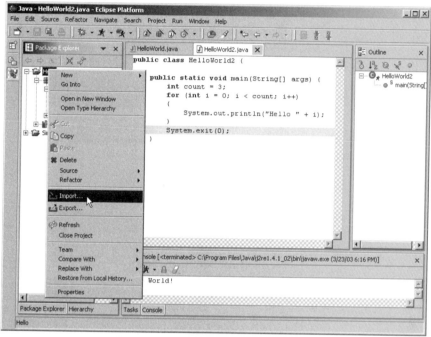

Figure 8.13: Import into the Hello project.

❑ **8.2(h) Select File system and click Next.**

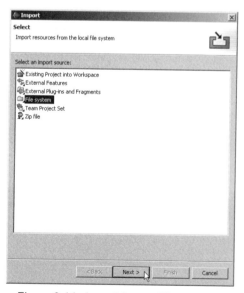

Figure 8.14: Import from a File system.

□ **8.2(i) Use the dropdown for the directory field to select D:\Source\Step 7.**

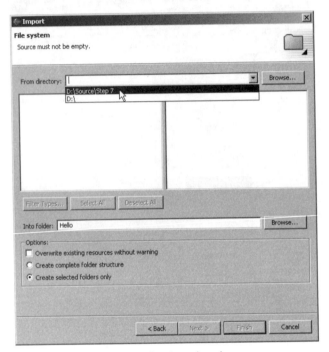

Figure 8.15: Using the directory dropdown.

Note: If you haven't already imported Step 7, you may not see anything in your dropdown, so instead just type "D:\Source\Step 7" into the Directory field and press the Tab key.

❑ **8.2(j) Left-click on the Step 7 folder.**

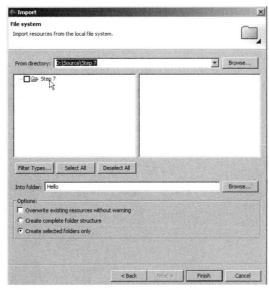

Figure 8.16: Select the Step 7 folder by left-clicking on it.

❑ **8.2(k) Check the checkbox next to HelloWorld2.java.**

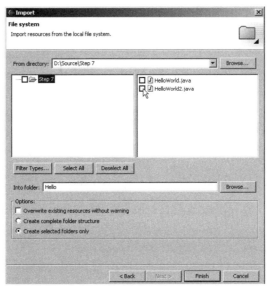

Figure 8.17: Click on the checkbox next to HelloWorld2.java to select it.

❑ **8.2(l) Click Finish.**

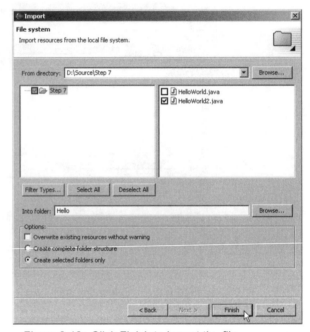

Figure 8.18: Click Finish to import the file.

If you have already followed the actions in Option 1, you'll get a confirmation dialog.

❑ **8.2(m) Select Yes to overwrite the existing HelloWorld2.java file.**

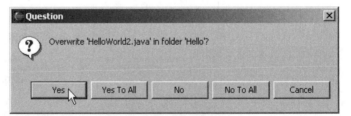

Figure 8.19: Overwrite the existing source.

If you didn't follow Option 1, you'll need to open the file.

❑ **8.2(n) Right-click on HelloWorld2.java and select Open.**

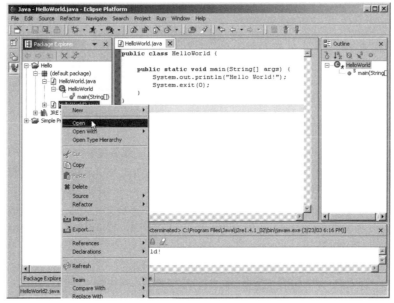

Figure 8.20: Open HelloWorld2.java with the popup menu.

And here is your open file!

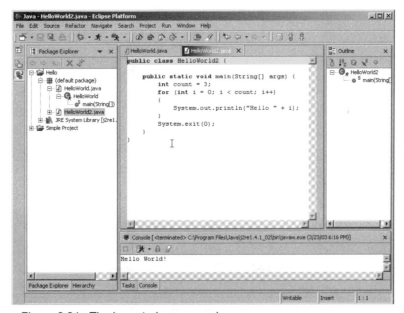

Figure 8.21: The imported source code.

Step 8.3—Run HelloWorld2

> **GOAL**
>
> You will now run the
> program you entered in Step 8.2.

It's time to use a little shortcut. Back in Step 8.1 you used the Run… option from the Run tool's dropdown. In subsequent steps, you selected all the defaults, and that was sufficient to run the program. Well, there's a quicker way to do all that. Use the Run As submenu and select the Java Application option. This will run the selected program as a Java Application with all the defaults. Let's do that now and watch how it works.

❑ **8.3(a) Left-click on HelloWorld2.java to select it.**

❑ **8.3(b) From the Run tool dropdown, select Run As/Java Application.**

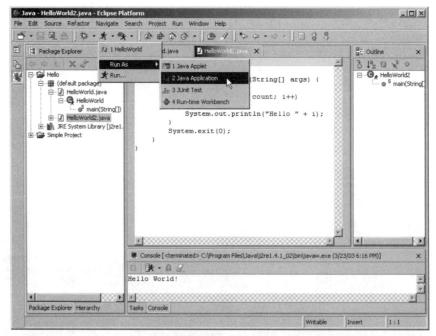

Figure 8.22: Use the Java Application option of the Run As submenu to quickly run HelloWorld2 with the default settings.

Note: Now that you've run the HelloWorld program and created the HelloWorld launch configuration, that configuration shows in the Run tool's dropdown list for easy access. As you add more configurations, they will be added as well, each with a number. The one marked number "1" will be the one selected if you just hit the Run tool button itself.

So you see the output as shown below. However, since there's very little real estate given over to the Console view, you might want to expand it. As always, to expand a view you just double-click on the title bar.

❑ **8.3(c) Double-click on the Console view title bar.**

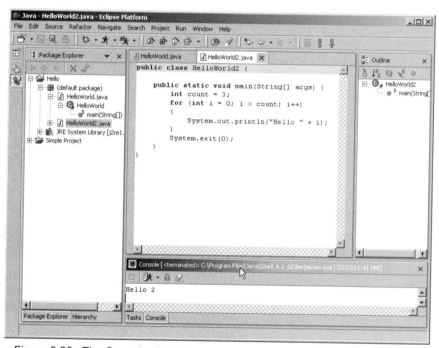

Figure 8.23: The Console view is a little cramped, so double-click on the title bar to expand it.

You'll see a view like the one in Figure 8.24. Notice that there are three "Hello" lines: Hello 0, Hello 1 and Hello 2, because you set the initial count to 3.

Double-click on the title bar again to restore the display to its original view.

❑ **8.3(d) Double-click on the title bar again.**

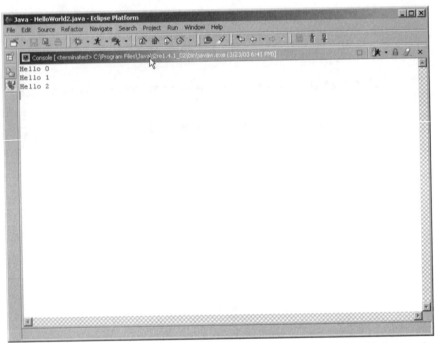

Figure 8.24: The Console view maximized. Double-clicking on the title bar again will restore the display.

We're back to the original view, as shown in Figure 8.25. Okay, you've accomplished both editing and running. Now it's time for the last step in development—debugging.

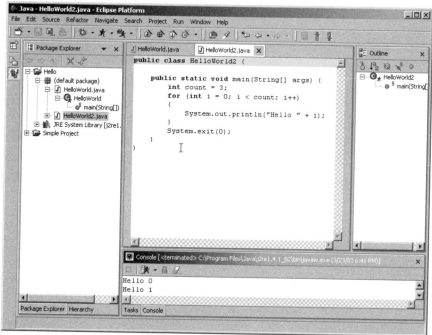

Figure 8.25: The display restored.

Step 8.4—Breakpointing a program

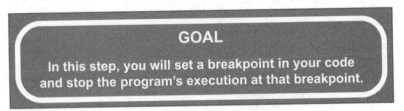

GOAL

In this step, you will set a breakpoint in your code and stop the program's execution at that breakpoint.

Setting a breakpoint is quite easy (although it takes some fine motor control). You'll notice a gray column to the left of your source code in the editor. That is the breakpoint, or debug, column. If you right-click in that column just to the left of the desired source code line, a popup menu will appear, allowing you to, among other things, add a breakpoint. If a breakpoint already exists at that location, you will be able to remove or modify it (for example, enabling the breakpoint on a specific condition). Since no breakpoint exists, the Add Breakpoint option will be enabled. Select it to add the new breakpoint.

❑ **8.4(a) Right-click on the debug column to the left of the for loop.**

❑ **8.4(b) Select Add Breakpoint.**

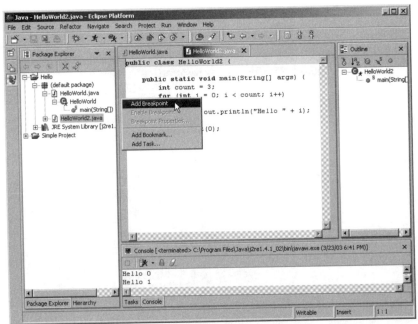

Figure 8.26: Click on the gray column next to your for loop and select Add Breakpoint.

Note: A small blue ball will appear next to the line that has a breakpoint. However, setting a breakpoint is not sufficient to debug a program. You must also run the program in debug mode. This is done by using the Debug tool rather than the Run tool.

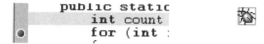

To run the program in debug mode, you use the Debug tool in the main tool bar. The Debug tool works very much like the Run tool; it remembers the last thing you ran and assumes that you will be running the same thing this time. So, since the last thing you ran was indeed HelloWorld2, you can now just press the Debug tool.

To be sure you are running the right program, roll your mouse over the Debug tool, and you'll see the tool tip pop up with the text "Debug HelloWorld2". If it does not, you can always use the Debug dropdown, which works the same way as the Run tool's dropdown.

❑ **8.4(c) Click the Debug tool button.**

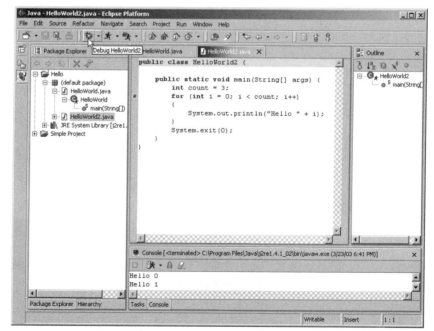

Figure 8.27: The Debug tool will default to the last thing you ran, which in this case is HelloWorld2.

Things now get interesting! Where in the world did all these windows come from? Well, this is the Debug perspective, which I introduced you to in Step 6. It is now here in full force, with all the windows full of goodies.

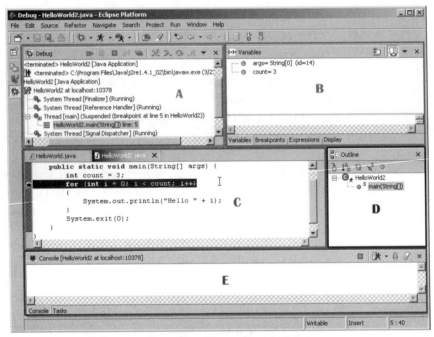

Figure 8.28: The many views of the Debug perspective.

Figure 8.28 shows the default Debug perspective, with five windows. The bottom three are actually brought over from the Java perspective, but the top two are brand new.

A. The Debug window, which shows the state of all processes, living or dead, on the machine.

B. The Display window. This particular window has several stacked views that you can use to interact with the program. By default, it shows the Variables view.

C., D., & E. The Editor, Outline, and Console views. These are actually all from the Java perspective, just resized and repositioned a bit.

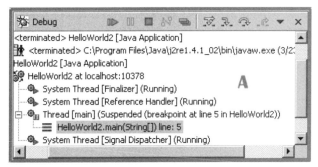

Figure 8.29: The Debug view.

The Debug view shows the various processes running (or no longer running). You can see the current one, which starts at the third line down, marked "HelloWorld2 [Java Application]". You'll see several threads, including three marked System Thread and one marked just Thread [main]. That one has an additional notation, (Suspended (breakpoint at line 5 in HelloWorld2)). which indicates that the thread is stopped at a breakpoint. Line 5 is the breakpoint, and you'll see that line indicated in the source display (Editor view) by a small blue arrow.

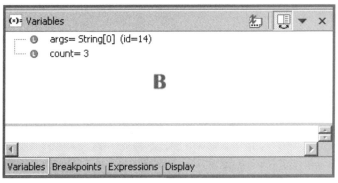

Figure 8.30: The Variables view.

This view shows the variables. You can not only inspect the contents of any variable; you can also interact with them, changing the contents. You will use this view in a moment to change the count variable. The Variables view shares this window with several other views. The Breakpoints view is used to manage breakpoints, and the Expressions and Display views can be used to do more detailed analysis of variables, even invoking methods if necessary.

Step 8.5—Modifying a Variable and Continuing

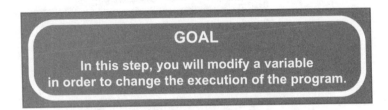

What I'd like you to do is to change the program so that it loops five times rather than three. How would you go about doing that? Well, the easiest way would be to change the count variable to the value 5, so let's do that.

❑ **8.5(a) Double-click on the count variable in the Variables view.**

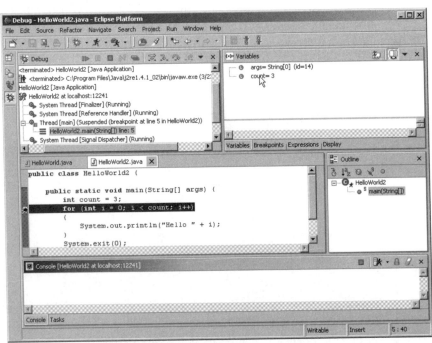

Figure 8.31: Double-click on the count variable to modify it.

A dialog will pop up, as shown in Figure 8.32.

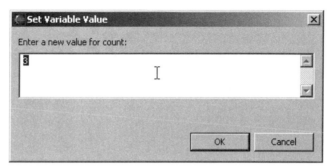

Figure 8.32: The Set Variable dialog.

Use this dialog to change the value to 5.

❏ **8.5(b) Enter the value 5 and click OK.**

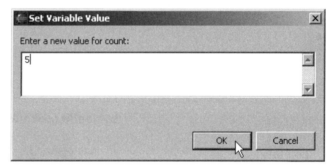

Figure 8.33: Updating the value.

You'll be returned to the workbench, where you will see that the value of the count variable has been changed to 5.

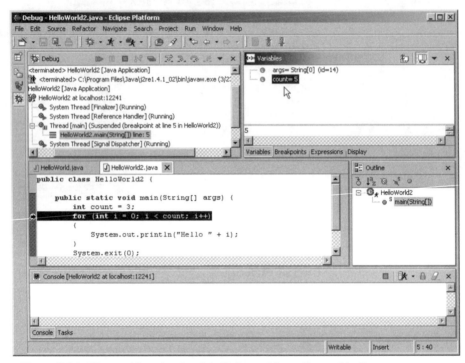

Figure 8.34: The workbench, showing that count has changed to 5.

The last thing to do now is to restart the program and let it execute with the new value. There are several tool buttons in the Debug view that will allow you to single-step, step into a function, step out of a function, and so on. In this case, you simply want the program to resume execution (and presumably to finish). You can do this by using the Resume tool, as shown in Figure 8.35.

❏ **8.5(c) Click the Resume tool to continue execution of the program.**

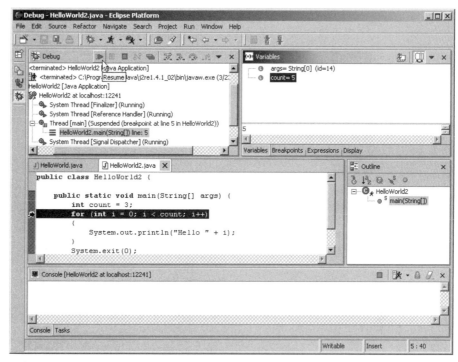

Figure 8.35: The Resume tool of the Debug view will resume execution from the current point.

And the result? As you can see in Figure 8.36, the program now executes its loop five times, printing Hello 3 and Hello 4. This is exactly what we wanted to have happen, and thus our debugging was a success!

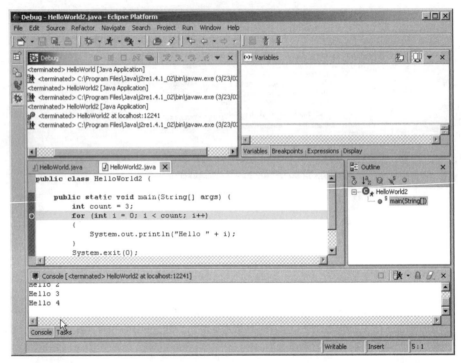

Figure 8.36: The modified execution of the program, showing the two additional lines of output.

So now that you've managed to enter source code, run a program, set a breakpoint, and modify the execution, you're ready to use the tool to do some real programming. In the next two steps, you will build a simple user interface and then connect it to a database. By the time you are done, you will have built a functioning application!

Before we exit here, though, we have one last thing to do: return to the Java perspective. I think the easiest way will be to close the Debug perspective. Use the Perspective Bar on the left of the workbench.

❑ **8.5(d) Right-click on Debug in the Perspective bar and select Close.**

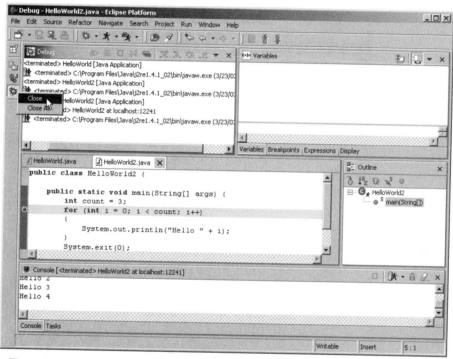

Figure 8.37: Closing the Debug perspective using the Perspective Bar.

This will close the Debug perspective and return you to the last open perspective, the Java perspective, as shown in Figure 8.38.

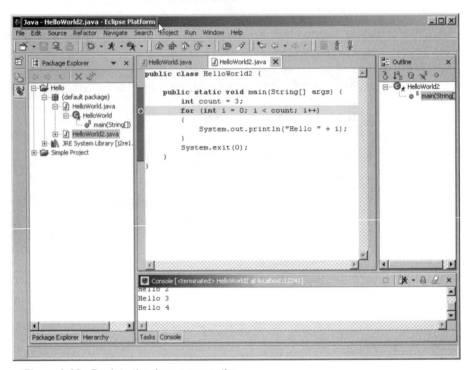

Figure 8.38: Back to the Java perspective.

Okay, you've written, run, and debugged a very simple application. Time to put a little more meat on it. First, a user interface: that's the task for Step 9.

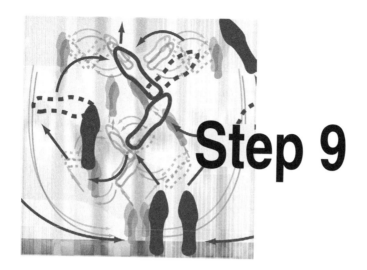

Step 9

The user interface

Next, you need a user interface. This step will create a very simple user interface that will prompt for an item number and return a description. The business logic portion will be completely simulated; you'll write a method that just does a lookup against a hardcoded list of item numbers. You'll add the database interaction in Step 10.

Overview—The thick client interface

Java has a number of options when it comes to user interfaces. One of the first tasks in any development project is to determine the interface (or interfaces) that will be required. In this book, you will be using a *thick client* interface-that is, one in which the majority of the user interface (UI) code runs on the client in a specially designed program. The UI is graphical in nature, supporting drag and drop, menu bars, and so on, like any typical Windows (or Macintosh or Gnome) application.

You'll use a thick client because it is the simplest to implement. There are no requirements for a Web application server as there would be with a browser-based interface.

Just because you've selected a thick client doesn't mean your job is over yet. Now you must decide which thick client interface to use. In earlier versions of Java, you chose between AWT (the Abstract Widget Toolkit) and Swing, but those days are gone, with Swing having all but completely replaced AWT in the general Java community.

But there is a newcomer, IBM's SWT, or Standard Widget Toolkit. SWT was designed to allow a faster, more native interface—Swing, especially in early releases, was notoriously slow and not particularly appealing visually. Since then, strides have been made, but IBM chose to invent its own wheel for the Eclipse project, and thus were SWT and its companion technology, JFace, born.

This chapter is not the place to debate the pros and cons of SWT and Swing. You can read all manner of opposing viewpoints in the various forums, and I address the issue in a little more detail in SideStep 4. However, for the purposes of this book, since Eclipse is our focus I thought I would also introduce you to the UI that Eclipse uses, namely SWT.

Step 9.1—Workbench cleanup

GOAL

This step just cleans up some of the open windows.

❑ **9.1(a) Close HelloWorld2.java by clicking on the X in the editor tab.**

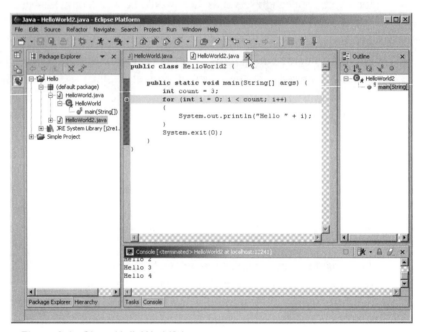

Figure 9.1: Close HelloWorld2.java.

❑ **9.1(b) Close HelloWorld.java by clicking on the X in the editor tab.**

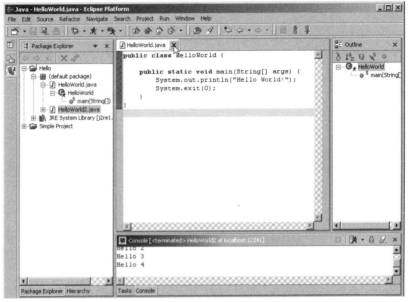

Figure 9.2: Close HelloWorld.java.

Note: The Console view shows the current console, which contains the results of the last debug run. To clear the current console, click on the "eraser" icon (the top icon on the right). The console view keeps the contents of all your recent runs. You can access a list of all console views by clicking the down arrow next to the running man icon (left of the eraser).

❑ **9.1(c) Clear the Console view.**

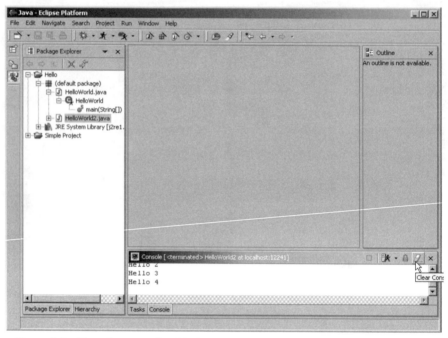

Figure 9.3: Clear the console with the eraser icon.

This will leave you with a nice, clean workbench like the one in Figure 9.4.

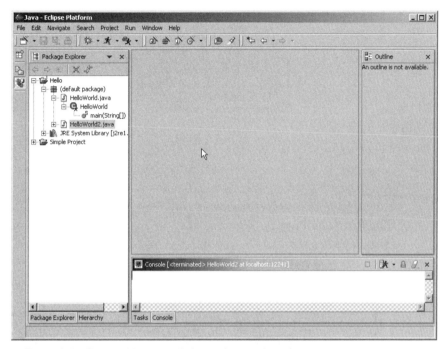

Figure 9.4: The workbench, all cleaned up and ready to go.

Step 9.2—Create a new project

GOAL

Create a new project
to hold the user interface programs.

The easiest way to avoid clutter is to segregate programs into projects. In this case, we'll create a new project called SWT, since we'll be concentrating on SWT programming. In previous steps, I had you add a new project by using the popup menu from the navigator view. In this step, I'll show you an alternative method: the File/New/Project... option. The File menu has a New submenu, and the New submenu has a Project... option.

❑ **9.2(a) From the Eclipse main menu bar, select File/New/Project . . .**

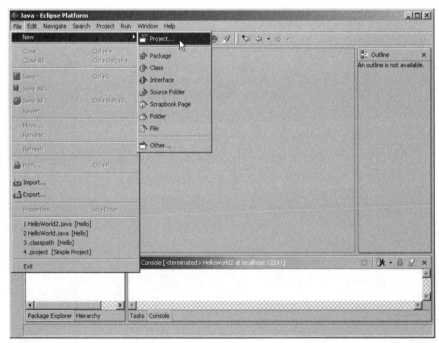

Figure 9.5: Adding a new project using the File menu, New submenu, Project. . . option.

❏ **9.2(b) Make sure Java and Java Project are selected and click Next.**

Figure 9.6: Adding a new Java Project.

❏ **9.2(c) Enter SWT in the Project name field and select Finish.**

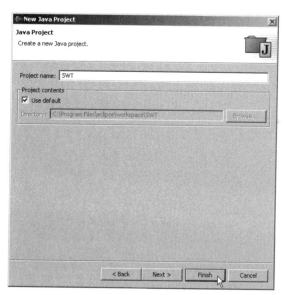

Figure 9.7: Enter the project name, SWT, and select the Finish button.

You will have added a new project, as shown in Figure 9.8.

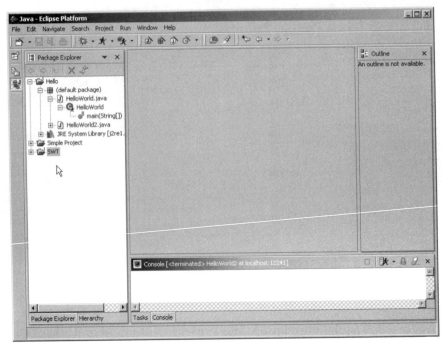

Figure 9.8: The new SWT project!

❑ **9.2(d) Expand the SWT project.**

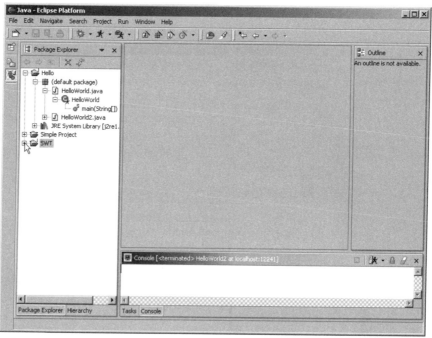

Figure 9.9: Use the plus sign to expand the SWT project.

You'll see a JAR file in your project. Roll your cursor over it as shown in Figure 9.10, and you'll see that it's the same runtime JAR file as in the Hello project.

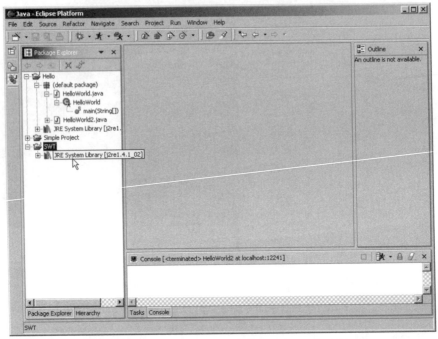

Figure 9.10: Rolling your cursor over the JAR file shows that it is the same runtime file as in the Hello project.

Step 9.3—Add a new class, HelloSWT

Like most third-party packages, the SWT packages are in a JAR file. SWT is a little different from other packages, though, in that it is not "100% Pure Java," meaning that there is at least one component to the SWT package that is not contained in a JAR file. For SWT, this is a special file that interfaces between the Java classes and the operating system. In Windows, this is a DLL file. In this step, you'll see one way of including this (or any other) DLL in your environment. Later we'll show you a more pervasive way.

❑ **9.3(a) Make sure the SWT project is selected.**

❑ **9.3(b) Right-click in the Package Explorer and select File/New/Class.**

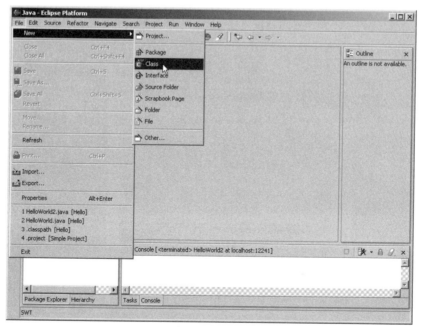

Figure 9.11: Creating a new class using New/Class.

❏ **9.3(c) Make sure the Source Folder is SWT.**

❏ **9.3(d) Leave Package blank.**

❏ **9.3(e) Leave Enclosing type unchecked.**

❏ **9.3(f) Enter HelloSWT in the Name field.**

❏ **9.3(g) Make sure public is checked, abstract and final unchecked.**

❏ **9.3(h) Leave Superclass as java.lang.Object, Interfaces blank.**

❏ **9.3(i) Make sure public static void main(String[] args) is checked.**

❏ **9.3(j) Leave the other two unchecked.**

❏ **9.3(k) Select Finish.**

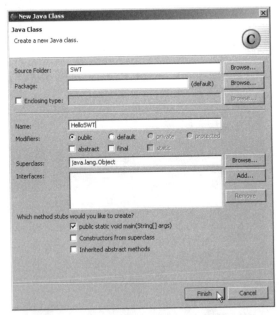

Figure 9.12: Setting the fields properly for a new class.

This will create a class HelloSWT in the default package (because you left Package blank) in project SWT. It will be a public class, neither abstract nor final. The class has no superclass (except for the implied superclass Object) and implements no interfaces. Finally, the IDE has been instructed to create a standard "main" method, but no other methods. That being the case, we will see the result as in Figure 9.13.

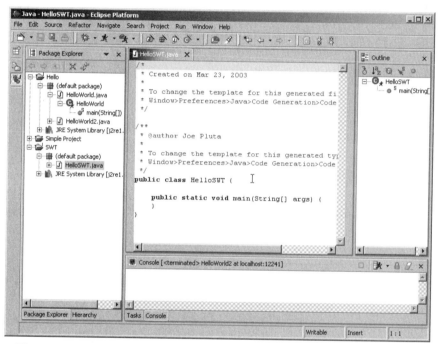

Figure 9.13: The result of the addition of the new class HelloSWT.

Step 9.4—Write the Code for the HelloSWT Class

> ## GOAL
>
> In this step, you'll enter just about
> the simplest SWT application possible.

You may either enter the code directly into the editor, or use the Import feature to import the source from the supplied CD-ROM. If you wish to enter the source yourself and get a feel for the source editor, use Option 1 below. Otherwise, skip ahead to Step 9.4(d), the instructions for Option 2.

Option 1—Source Entry

❑ **9.4(a) Enter the following source code after the comments.**

```java
import org.eclipse.swt.*;
import org.eclipse.swt.layout.*;
import org.eclipse.swt.widgets.*;

public class HelloSWT {

    public static void main(String[] args) {

        // Create a standard window
        Display display = new Display();
        Shell shell = new Shell(display);
        shell.setText("HelloSWT");

        // Final setup - set size and show the window
        shell.setSize(150, 50);
        shell.open();
        while (!shell.isDisposed()) {
            if (!display.readAndDispatch())
                display.sleep();
        }

        // When done, clean up resource and exit
        display.dispose();
    }
}
```

At this point, your screen will look like the one in Figure 9.14.

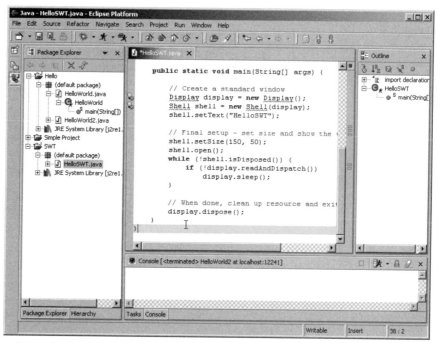

Figure 9.14: Source code entered into the editor pane.

Use the scroll bar to reposition the source to the top of the code. You can also use standard editing keystrokes, such as Ctrl-Home.

❏ 9.4(b) Position the window to the top of the source.

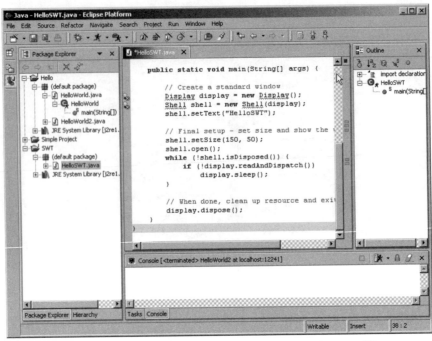

Figure 9.15: Using the scrollbar to position the window to the top of the source.

Now you can save the source. One way is to use the Save tool on the main Eclipse tool bar. You can also use Ctrl-S or the editor popup menu.

❑ 9.4(c) Click on the Save button on the toolbar.

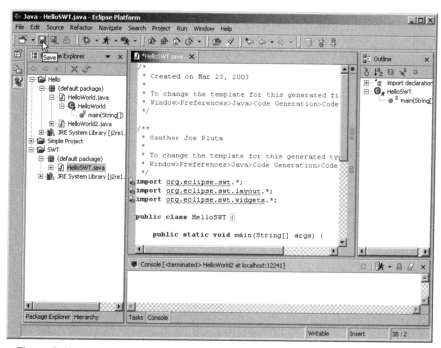

Figure 9.16: Using the Save tool to save the source.

You'll see the screen shown in Figure 9.17. You may skip ahead now to Step 9.5 (you may also perform Option 2 if you'd like, but there's really no need to do both options).

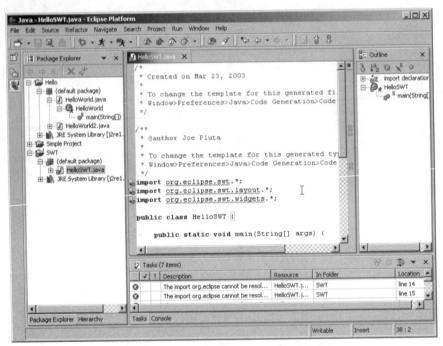

Figure 9.17: The workbench after saving the new HelloSWT source.

Option 2—Importing Source from CD

Here you'll perform nearly the same tasks as in Step 7; the only difference is the name of the file you'll be importing and the project you'll be importing it into.

❑ **9.4(d) Insert the supplied CD-ROM into your CD-ROM drive.**

❑ **9.4(e) Select the SWT project, then select File/Import . . . from the main menu bar.**

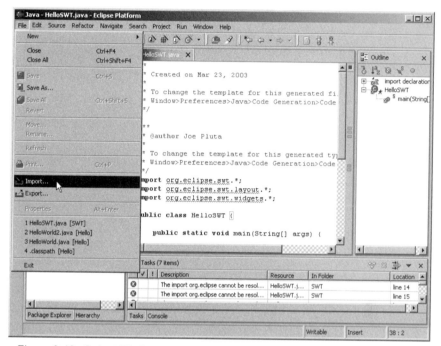

Figure 9.18: Select File/Import . . . to Import a file into the SWT project.

On the Import screen, you have many options as to your import source. Since your source is in a folder on the CD-ROM, you'll use the File system option.

❑ **9.4(f) Select File system and click Next.**

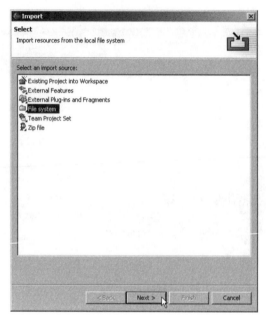

Figure 9.19: Select File system as the source for the import.

You need to specify the location of the files. Specify *R*:\Source\Step 9, where *R* is the letter of the CD-ROM drive where you loaded the disk. In Figure 9.20, the CD is loaded in the D: drive.

Note: Be sure that the Into folder field has a value of SWT. If it doesn't, then you didn't have the SWT project selected when you began the Import process. To fix the problem, just key in SWT.

❑ **9.4(g) Enter *R*:\Source\Step 9 in the From directory field, where *R* is the drive letter of your CD-ROM drive, and press the Tab key.**

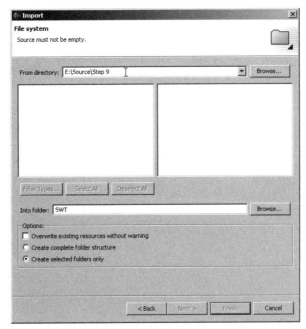

Figure 9.20: Enter R:\Source\Step 9, where R is the drive where you loaded the included CD-ROM.

The Tab key will cause the left pane to be loaded with an icon for the Source folder. Select the Source folder by clicking on it.

❑ **9.4(h) Left-click on the Step 9 folder.**

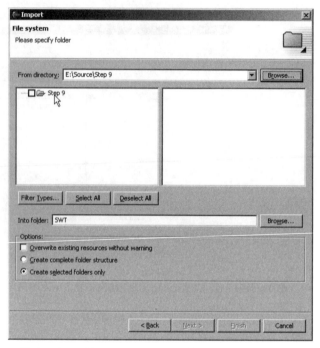

Figure 9.21: Select the Step 9 folder by left-clicking on it.

This will cause the contents of the Step 9 folder to appear in the right-hand pane, as shown in Figure 9.22.

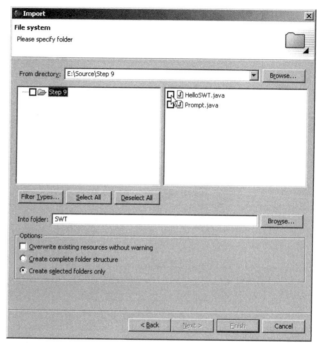

Figure 9.22: The contents of the Step 9 folder will appear in the right hand pane.

Select HelloSWT.java by clicking on its checkbox.

❑ **9.4(i) Select HelloSWT.java and click Finish.**

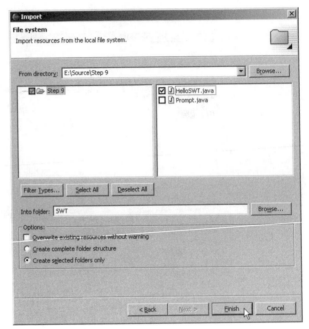

Figure 9.23: Select only HelloSWT.java, then click Finish.

You should see the following dialog box.

❑ **9.4(j) Select Yes on the confirmation box that pops up.**

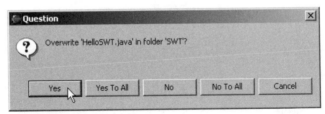

Figure 9.24: This prompt confirms that you really want to overwrite your source.

Your display should look just like the one shown in Figure 9.25.

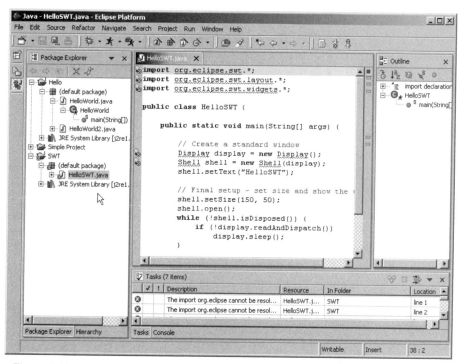

Figure 9.25: The workbench display after importing the source code. Note the red X's in the Package Explorer.

In the Package Explorer view, you should see small red boxes with X's in them overlying the icons for the SWT project, its default package, and the HelloSWT.java class. These indicate that there is at least one error in the HelloSWT.java class. Now you need to determine what is causing the error.

Step 9.5—Fixing import errors

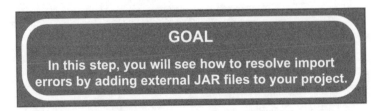

GOAL

In this step, you will see how to resolve import errors by adding external JAR files to your project.

I'm not going to go into detail about the SWT packages in this step. I'll cover them a little more closely in the following steps, but even so, this book is not meant to be an SWT tutorial, but more of a simple introduction. I'll leave the heavy details of SWT to another book.

In this step, I just want to show you a few things about handling errors in Eclipse.

Figure 9.26 shows a typical editing display, with a few errors. Unlike most cases, this particular class has only one problem: It can't find its JAR files. But before I get into that too much, I'd like to point out a few things.

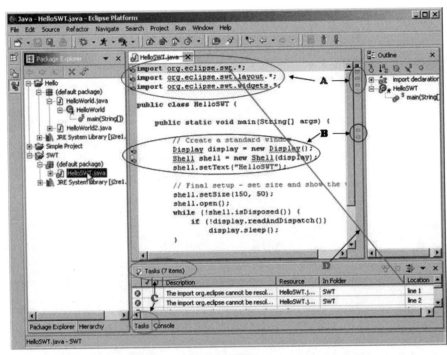

Figure 9.26: The Java editor with several errors.

A. Note how there are three lines in error in this group. Eclipse identifies them with a white X in a red circle, in this case directly to the left of the line in error. The part of the line that is actually causing the error is underlined with a squiggly red line, just as Microsoft Word underlines misspelled words. This underline is sometimes called a scribble. Also notice that the rightmost column of the edit pane contains a number of small pink rectangles. Each rectangle corresponds to an error in the source, and each one appears based on it's the error's position in the source file. The earlier the error occurs in the source, the higher it is on the error bar.

Note: You can also use these rectangles as navigation devices—click on one to position the source containing the error.

B. These two errors also have scribbles and corresponding rectangles in the error bar.

C. Here's an interesting thing that happened while we weren't looking: This window changed itself from the Console view to the Tasks view. The Tasks view is commonly used to display errors from the other views. The Eclipse designers thought it important to "pop up" the Tasks view whenever an error occurs, to show you the current errors.

D. Each line in the Tasks view represents an error in the source code. All errors are collected in this view (and in fact, you can add your own tasks into the view, as sort of a dynamic to-do list). The Resource and Folder columns tell you which resource the error pertains to, while the Location column tells you where in the resource the error occurs. These lines also act as another navigation device—by clicking on a line, the editor will be positioned automatically to the corresponding error.

So, by either using the error bar of the editor pane or clicking on an error in the Tasks view, you can position the editor to show the error. In this case, you already have the errors visible in the editor pane, so you can simply go in and correct them.

Before we start fixing things, I'd like to do one extra cleanup step. This will just remove a bit of clutter in the Package Explorer pane.

❑ 9.5(a) Collapse the Hello project.

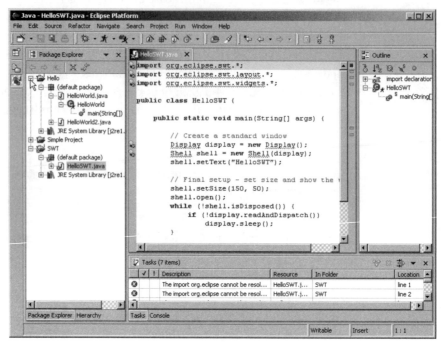

Figure 9.27: Collapse the Hello project by left-clicking the minus sign.

Now you have the view in Figure 9.28.

Okay, the workbench is a little clearer and you can begin fixing errors. First, you need to know what those errors are. An easy way is to roll your mouse pointer over the red circle in the left-hand column of the editor pane.

❏ **9.5(b) Roll your mouse pointer over the error icon to see the popup of the full error description.**

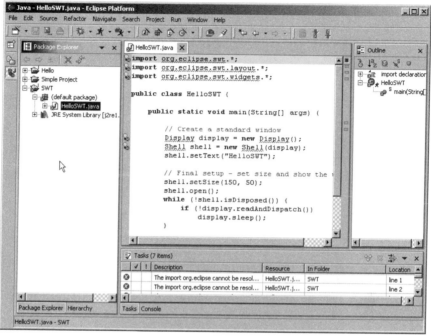

Figure 9.28: A slightly less cluttered Package Explorer.

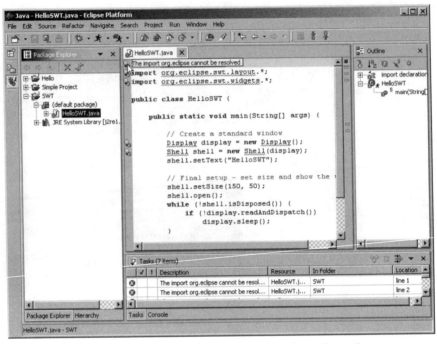

Figure 9.29: Rolling your cursor over the error icon shows the entire error description in a popup.

In this case, the error is very straightforward: "The import org.eclipse cannot be resolved." This indicates that the compiler is unable to find the package org.eclipse in any of the JAR files in its classpath. To fix this error, you must include the appropriate JAR file.

External JAR files for a project are set in the Properties dialog. So are many other project attributes. The Properties dialog is very important for just about every level of resource in the Eclipse environment, so you when you have spare time, you may want to explore the various Properties dialogs.

Note: Getting to the Properties for a project is the same as for any other resource: Right-click and select Properties. You can also use the File/Properties menu option from the main Eclipse menu bar, or you can select a resource and press Alt-Enter.

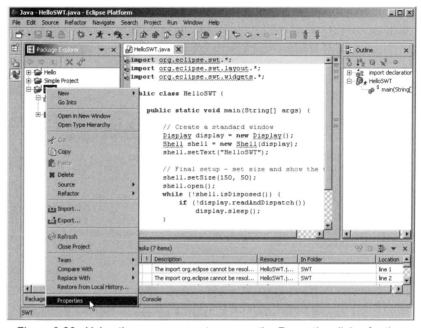

Figure 9.30: Using the popup menu to access the Properties dialog for the SWT project.

The classpath is under the Java Build Path properties.

❏ **9.5(c) Select Java Build Path in the Properties dialog box.**

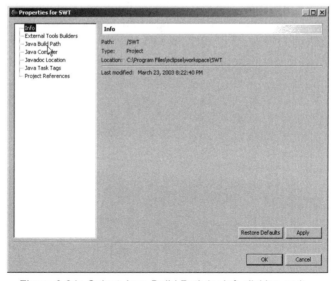

Figure 9.31: Select Java Build Path by left-clicking on it.

Almost there . . . the classpath is maintained in the Libraries tab.

❑ 9.5(d) Select the Libraries tab.

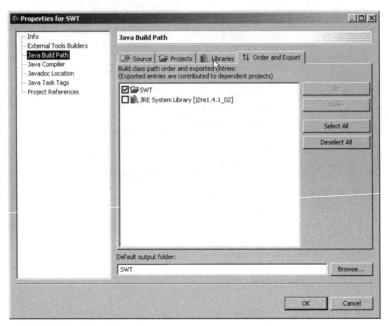

Figure 9.32: Select the Libraries tab by left-clicking on it.

At this point you can do a number of things. You may add JARs from within your workspace, define variables, add folders, and so on. For more information on this and any other dialog, press the F1 key for help. For this project, though, you need a JAR file that is not in your workspace—that is, an external JAR file.

❏ **9.5(e) Click Add External JARs . . .**

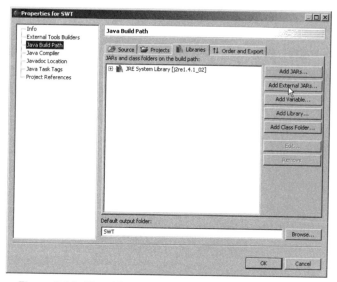

Figure 9.33: To add a JAR file that is not in your workspace, press Add External JARs . . .

A standard file finder dialog will appear. First, navigate to your primary Eclipse folder. This is the folder "eclipse" within your Eclipse install directory, which you saved as $ECLIPSEINST in Step 2.1(h). Then open the subfolder plugins.

❏ **9.5(f) Open the folder named plugins.**

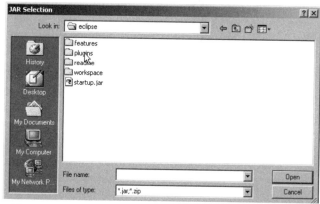

Figure 9.34: Open the plugins folder by double-clicking on it or selecting it and pressing Enter.

Next, you need to get to the SWT folder. It will have a different name depending on the platform and version, but it will start with "org.eclipse.swt," then end with the platform and version.

❏ **9.5(g) Open the folder named org.eclipse.swt.win32_2.1.0.**

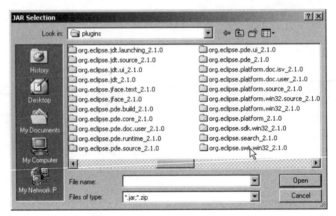

Figure 9.35: Open the org.eclipse.swt.win32_2.1.0 folder.

❏ **9.5(h) Open the folder named ws.**

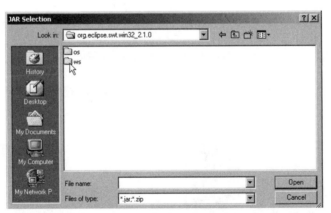

Figure 9.36: Open the ws folder.

❏ **9.5(i) Open the folder named win32.**

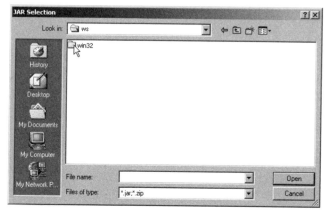

Figure 9.37: Open the win32 folder.

Finally, you will have reached a point where you see a JAR file named swt.jar. This is the JAR file that you want to include on your classpath.

❏ **9.5(j) Open the file named swt.jar.**

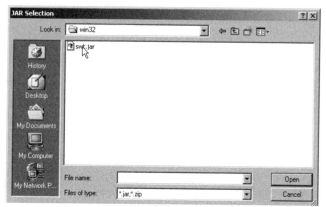

Figure 9.38: Open swt.jar to include it in the classpath.

You'll see that the JAR file has been added to the Libraries tab. Just select OK to continue.

❑ **9.5(k) Click OK.**

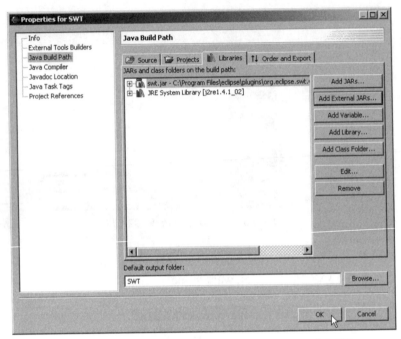

Figure 9.39: The new JAR file is in the Libraries tab, so click OK.

Your workbench should now look like the one in Figure 9.40. Notice that all the red X's are gone. There are a couple of yellow exclamation points instead. Actually, this icon consists of a light bulb *and* an exclamation point. The light bulbs mean you can click on the error to get a hint. The exclamation points indicate warnings; they are also in the Tasks view.

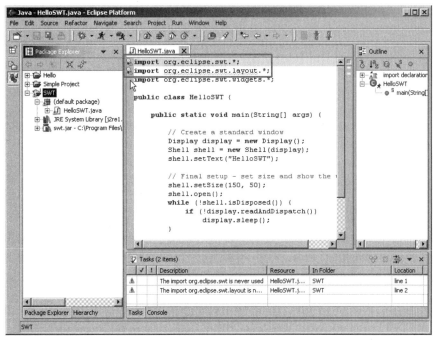

Figure 9.40: The errors have been replaced with warnings.

Just as with errors, you can get the entire text for a warning to pop up by rolling the cursor over it, as shown in Figure 9.41.

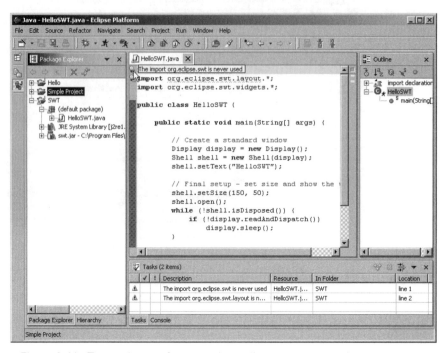

Figure 9.41: To see the text for a warning, roll your cursor over it.

In this case, the warning is that the import is never used. That's actually a fairly new warning message. As late as release 2.1M4 of Eclipse, this condition wasn't even flagged. But it's nice to know; you can remove the extraneous imports if you care to.

In any event, you have now fixed all the fatal errors. You can remove the imports to remove the warning messages if you'd like, or you can simply go on to Step 9.6.

Step 9.6—Running the HelloSWT class

You're going to find that there is one additional requirement for running an SWT application: You must add the native library to your runtime environment. In Linux that would be a shared library, but in Windows you use a DLL. In this step I'll show you a rather nonintrusive way to include a DLL; this method is best used when a new DLL is being tested.

In a later step I'll show you how to reconfigure your machine so that you don't have to modify each individual launch configuration. So far, I haven't even mentioned what the code does. Let's get it to run, and then I'll review the source in a little more detail. First, try to run the class. This time, you'll use the Run menu from the Eclipse main menu bar.

❑ **9.6(a) Select the HelloSWT class by left-clicking on it.**

❑ **9.6(b) From the main menu bar, select Run/Run As/Java Application.**

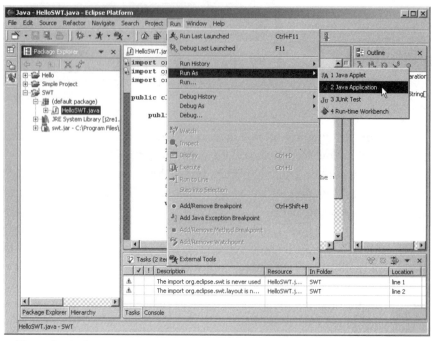

Figure 9.42: Running HelloSWT as a Java Application.

This will create a launch configuration for HelloSWT with the default characteristics and then attempt to run it.

Unfortunately, you won't meet with a lot of success, as you can see in Figure 9.43. And, since the Console view is rather small, it's not easy to see the error.

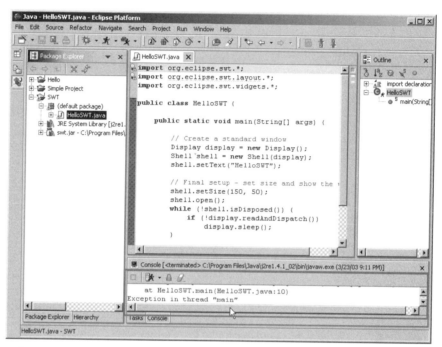

Figure 9.43: Red text is a good sign that an error occurred, but it's hard to see exactly what the error is.

The easiest way to see the error is to expand the Console view. Like any other view, you can expand the Console by double-clicking its title bar.

❏ **9.6(c) Double-click on the Console view's title bar to expand it.**

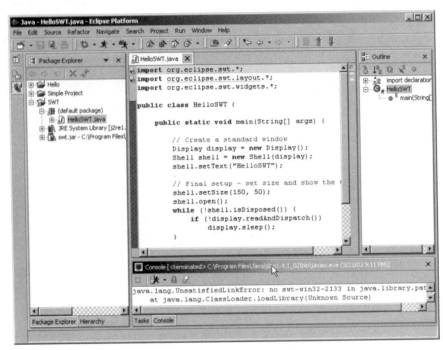

Figure 9.44: Double-click on the Console view's title bar.

You will see the display shown in Figure 9.45. Note the error highlighted in the figure.

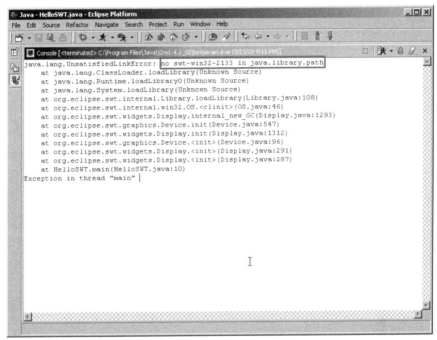

Figure 9.45: And here is the error—an UnsatisfiedLinkError.

This is an UnsatisfiedLinkError, which indicates that the Java Virtual Machine (JVM) was unable to find the implementation of a native method. As I explained at the beginning of this step, you need to include the native library in your runtime environment.

Restore the Console view to its normal size by double-clicking on the title-bar again.

❑ **9.6(d) Double-click on the Console view title bar to return it to normal.**

Adding the library to your runtime environment is accomplished by adding a runtime switch to your JVM. This is done in your launch configuration. But before you can do that, you need to know what switch to add. The switch is of the following format:

```
-Djava.library.path=$LIBPATH
```

The contents of the $LIBPATH variable depend on the operating system, the version of Eclipse, and where you installed it. In Step 2.1(h) I had you write down a value called $ECLIPSEINST, which was the directory you extracted Eclipse into. For example, I am using Windows and I installed Eclipse in "C:\Program Files," so my $ECLIPSEINST is "C:\Program Files." When you use a file extraction utility to extract the Eclipse files from the ZIP file, it creates another folder named "eclipse" under your install folder. This is now your "base" folder. We'll call that $ECLIPSE.

Eclipse by default is installed under your install folder in a folder called "eclipse," so the base folder is $ECLIPSEINST\eclipse. Let's call this the base Eclipse path, $ECLIPSE.

❏ **9.6(e) Save the base path as $ECLIPSE: _____.**

You now need to find the folder containing the native library and the name of that library (actually, the library will be used a little later, but it's best to do the work now and save the results for later). In Windows, you can use the Window command line to find this information, as shown on the following page.

❏ **9.6(f) Start a Windows command line and execute the following commands.**

You can do this by going to the Start menu, selecting Run…, and then typing in the value "cmd" and pressing Enter. This will start a command line. Then follow the script below (you type in the portions in bold):

```
Microsoft Windows 2000 [Version 5.00.2195]
(C) Copyright 1985-2000 Microsoft Corp.

C:\>cd c:\Program Files\eclipse

C:\Program Files\eclipse>cd plugins

C:\Program Files\eclipse\plugins>dir *swt*
 Volume in drive C is Local Disk
 Volume Serial Number is 88F5-29E7
```

```
Directory of C:\Program Files\eclipse\plugins

03/28/2003  04:25p      <DIR>          org.eclipse.swt.win32_2.1.0
03/28/2003  04:25p      <DIR>          org.eclipse.swt_2.1.0
               0 File(s)              0 bytes
               2 Dir(s)  31,234,199,552 bytes free

C:\Program Files\eclipse\plugins>cd org.eclipse.swt.win32_2.1.0

C:\Program Files\eclipse\plugins\org.eclipse.swt.win32_2.1.0>cd os\win32\ 86

C:\Program Files\eclipse\plugins\org.eclipse.swt.win32_2.1.0\os\win32\x86>dir
Volume in drive C is Local Disk
Volume Serial Number is 88F5-29E7

Directory of C:\Program Files\eclipse\plugins\org.eclipse.swt.win32_2.1.0\os\wi
n32\x86

03/28/2003  04:25p      <DIR>          .
03/28/2003  04:25p      <DIR>          ..
03/27/2003 100:01p        278,528 swt-win32-2133.dll
               1 File(s)        278,528 bytes
               2 Dir(s)  31,234,199,552 bytes free
```

1. cd c:\Program Files\eclipse
   (this is your $ECLIPSE base directory from Step 2.1(h))

2. cd plugins
   (changes to the plugins folder)

3. dir *swt*
   (lists everything with "swt" in it)

4. At this point, you'll see a directory. Copy down the value with "win32" in it
   (this is the value $LIBVERSION)

5. cd org.eclipse.swt.win32_2.1.0
   (this is $LIBVERSION from Step 4)

6. cd os\win32\x86
   (this gets you to the Windows32/Intel folder)

7. dir

8. Another directory. Copy the name of the file in it.
   (this is the value $LIBNAME)

So, on my machine, the values are as follows:

$ECLIPSE	c:\Program Files\eclipse
$LIBVERSION	org.eclipse.swt.win32_2.1.0
$LIBNAME	swt-win32-2133.dll

The $LIBPATH value is simply a folder. On a Windows machine, the value is

$ECLIPSE\plugins\$LIBVERSION\os\win32\x86.

On my machine, that makes it the following:

C:\Program Files\eclipse\plugins\org.eclipse.swt.win32_2.1.0\os\win32\x86

Your values should be very similar. Knowing them, you can now modify your launch configuration. You should double-check to make sure that $LIBNAME matches the name of the file that triggered the UnsatisfiedLinkError back in Figure 9.45. In my case, you can see that the name is swt-win32-2133 in both cases, so I definitely found the correct library. If these values don't match, then you have a configuration problem with your Eclipse environment. Chances are, though, that if you had that bad an environment, Eclipse wouldn't run at all, since Eclipse depends on SWT for its user interface.

❏ **9.6(g) Save the value for $LIBVERSION: _____.**

❏ **9.6(h) Save the value for $LIBNAME: _____.**

❏ **9.6(i) Save the value for $LIBPATH: _____.**

The next task is to modify the launch configuration. To do this, you need to bring up the list of launch configurations using the Run . . . option of the Run menu.

❏ **9.6(j) From the Eclipse main menu bar, select Run/Run . . .**

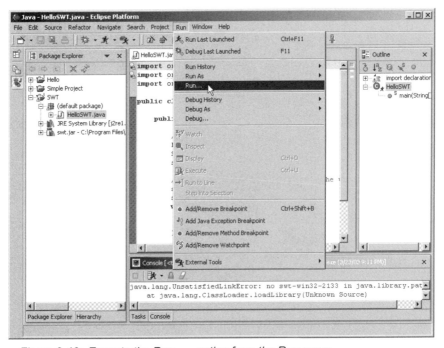

Figure 9.46: Execute the Run . . . option from the Run menu.

This brings up a list of launch configurations. HelloSWTshould already be selected, since it's the last one you ran. If not, select it. Now you want to modify the arguments passed to the JVM.

❏ 9.6(k) Select the Arguments tab.

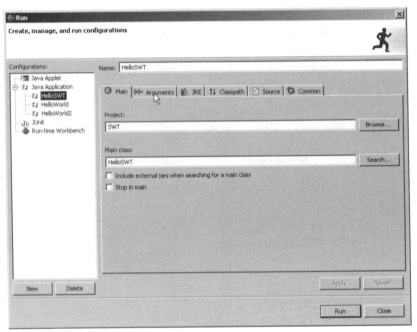

Figure 9.47: Left-click on the Arguments tab to select it.

There are two kinds of arguments: arguments passed to the program (which can be accessed via the args array in the main method) and arguments passed to the JVM (which affect how the JVM operates). This is a JVM argument, and is added to the box marked VM arguments. Remember, in 9.6(i) you wrote down the value for $LIBPATH. On my machine, it was

C:\Program Files\eclipse\plugins\org.eclipse.swt.win32_2.1.0\os\win32\x86

Add this to the VM arguments with the following formula:

```
"-Djava.library.path=$LIBPATH"
```

Remember to include the quotes, since you may have a space in one of your folder names.

❑ **9.6(l) Add the library path argument to the JVM and click Run.**

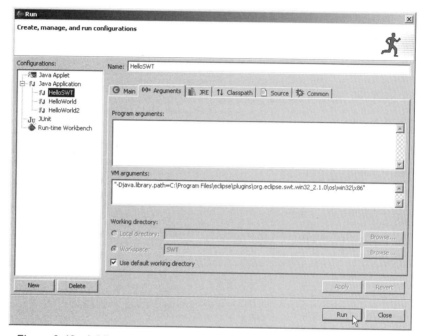

Figure 9.48: Adding the folder that contains the native library as a JVM argument.

Finally, you will see a small window pop up, as shown in Figure 9.49. There are no decorations; the only thing even slightly custom is the HelloSWT in the title bar, but it is nonetheless a real, complete SWT window.

Figure 9.49: Here is your SWT window!

After you've admired your handiwork for a while, close it, because there's a lot more work to do.

❑ **9.6(m) Close the window.**

Figure 9.50: Close the window using the X.

Note: You may still be having problems getting your program to run. If you continue to get the UnsatisfiedLinkError message, then you might have had a typo on Step 9.6(l). You can either try to fix it, or simply wait for Step 9.7, where I show you an alternative technique for setting up your runtime environment.

Code review: HelloSWT

```
import org.eclipse.swt.*;
import org.eclipse.swt.layout.*;
import org.eclipse.swt.widgets.*;
```

As you saw during editing, only one of these imports is actually needed, the one for org.eclipse.swt.widgets. The widgets package contains the definitions for most of the basic SWT classes, including Display and Shell.

```
public class HelloSWT {

    public static void main(String[] args) {
```

This is standard code for any runnable Java application, SWT or not.

```
// Create a standard window
Display display = new Display();
Shell shell = new Shell(display);
shell.setText("HelloSWT");
```

This is standard interface code. The Display object communicates with the operating system, while the Shell object defines the top-level window. The only "custom" code is the setText call, which sets the text of the title bar.

```
// Final setup - set size and show the window
shell.setSize(150, 50);
shell.open();
while (!shell.isDisposed()) {
        if (!display.readAndDispatch())
                display.sleep();
}
```

The setSize call sets the initial size of the window in pixels. After that, the window is opened and then the program goes into a standard event-dispatching loop (this is reminiscent of the earliest days of Windows or OS/2 GUI programming, where you handled each event yourself). This is what the primary thread for any SWT application does: sleep and dispatch.

```
            // When done, clean up resource and exit
            display.dispose();
        }
}
```

At this point, it disposes of the Display object, which releases any resources. This is one of the knocks on SWT; the programmer must manually release resources. For example, a Color object is a resource that must be released when no longer in use.

Step 9.7—Add a new class, Prompt

☐ **9.7(a) Make sure the SWT project is selected.**

☐ **9.7(b) Using the Eclipse main menu bar, select New/Class.**

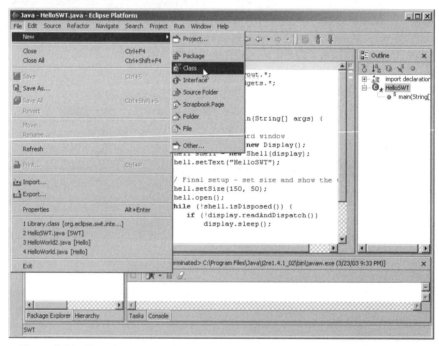

Figure 9.51: Creating a new class using the main menu bar's New/Class option.

❑ **9.7(c) Make sure the Source Folder is SWT'.**

❑ **9.7(d) Leave Package blank.**

❑ **9.7(e) Leave Enclosing type unchecked.**

❑ **9.7(f) Enter Prompt in the Name field.**

❑ **9.7(g) Make sure public is checked, abstract and final unchecked.**

❑ **9.7(h) Leave Superclass as java.lang.Object, Interfaces blank.**

❑ **9.7(i) Make sure public static void main(String[] args) is checked.**

❑ **9.7(j) Leave the other two unchecked.**

❑ **9.7(k) Select Finish.**

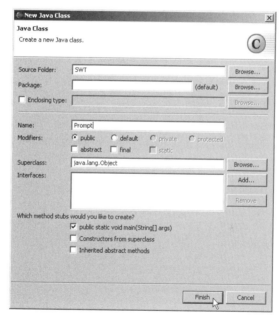

Figure 9.52: Setting the fields properly for a new class.

This will create a class Prompt in the default package (because you left package blank) in project SWT, as shown in Figure 9.53.

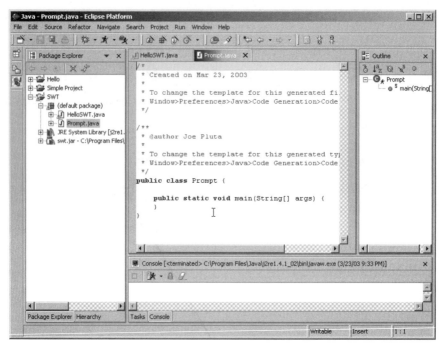

Figure 9.53: The result of the addition of the new class Prompt.

Step 9.8—Modify the new Prompt class

As usual, you can do this one of two ways: write the code or import the code. Option 1 is to modify the source manually. If you'd rather skip this step, go on to Option 2 to import the code.

Option 1—Source Entry

Enter the new code.

❑ **9.8(a) Enter the following source code after the comments.**

```java
import java.util.Hashtable;

import org.eclipse.swt.*;
import org.eclipse.swt.graphics.*;
import org.eclipse.swt.layout.*;
import org.eclipse.swt.widgets.*;

public class Prompt {

        // Resources
        Display display;
        Shell shell;
        Color red, white;

        // Fields
        Text f1;
        Label f2;

        public Prompt() {
        }

        public void run() {
                init();
                setLayout();
                createWidgets();
                show();
                cleanup();
        }
```

```
private void init() {
    // Create a standard window
    display = new Display();
    shell = new Shell(display);
    shell.setText("Prompt3");

    // Create some colors
    red = new Color(display, 255, 0, 0);
    white = new Color(display, 255, 255, 255);
}

private void setLayout() {
    // Create the layout for the widgets
    GridLayout grid = new GridLayout();
    grid.numColumns = 2;
    grid.makeColumnsEqualWidth = true;
    shell.setLayout(grid);
}

private void createWidgets() {
    // Create my widgets
    Label l1 = new Label(shell, SWT.NONE);
    l1.setText("Item Number:");

    f1 = new Text(shell, SWT.BORDER | SWT.SINGLE);
    f1.setTextLimit(20);

    Label l2 = new Label(shell, SWT.NONE);
    l2.setText("Description:");

    f2 = new Label(shell, SWT.NONE);
    f2.setText(" ");

    Button b1 = new Button(shell, SWT.PUSH);
    b1.setText("Find");
    b1.addListener(SWT.Selection, new Listener() {
        public void handleEvent(Event event) {
            doFind();
        }
    });

    Button b2 = new Button(shell, SWT.PUSH);
    b2.setText("Exit");
    b2.addListener(SWT.Selection, new Listener() {
        public void handleEvent(Event event) {
            doExit();
        }
    });
}
```

```java
private void doFind() {
    String desc = getDescription(f1.getText());
    if (desc == null)
    {
        f1.setForeground(white);
        f1.setBackground(red);
        f2.setText("Not Found");
        f2.setForeground(red);
    }
    else
    {
        f1.setForeground(null);
        f1.setBackground(null);
        f2.setText(desc);
        f2.setForeground(null);
    }
}

private void doExit() {
    shell.close();
}

private static final Hashtable items;
static {
    items = new Hashtable();
    items.put("DOG", "My Puppy");
    items.put("CAT", "My Kitty");
    items.put("OCTOPUS", "Calamari Kid");
}

private String getDescription(String item)
{
    return (String) items.get(item);
}

private void show() {
    // Final setup - size the display show it
    shell.setSize(200, 100);
    shell.open();
    while (!shell.isDisposed()) {
        if (!display.readAndDispatch())
            display.sleep();
    }
}
```

```
private void cleanup() {
    // When done, clean up resources
    display.dispose();
    red.dispose();
    white.dispose();
}


public static void main(String[] args) {
    new Prompt().run();
    System.exit(0);
}
}
```

❑ **9.8(b) Save the source code.**

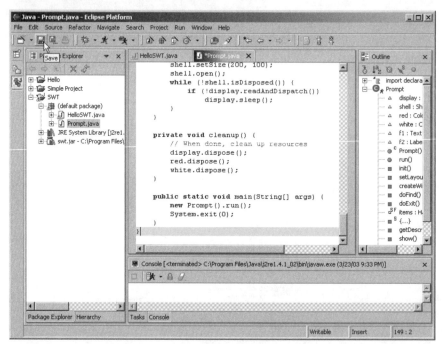

Figure 9.54: Save the source code. This figure shows the use of the Eclipse tool bar's Save tool.

❏ 9.8(c) Press Ctrl-Home.

Your display should now be similar to Figure 9.55.

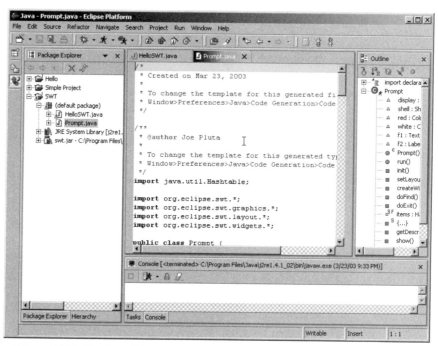

Figure 9.55: The top of the source code after you press Ctrl-Home.

Option 2—Importing Source from CD

☐ **9.8(d) Insert the supplied CD-ROM into your CD-ROM drive.**

☐ **9.8(e) Right-click on the SWT project and select Import . . .**

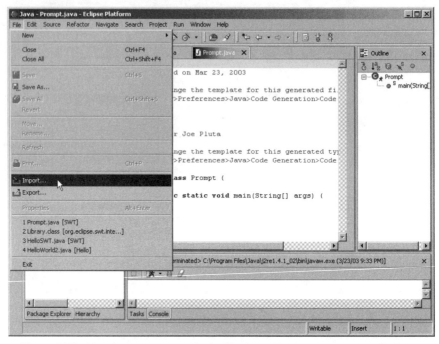

Figure 9.56: Use the popup menu in the Package Explorer to Import a file into the SWT project.

❏ **9.8(f) Select File system and click Next.**

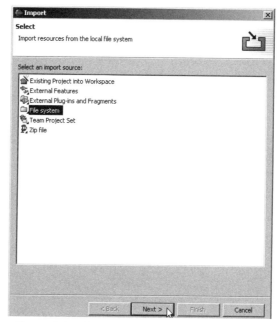

Figure 9.57: Select File system as the source for the import.

❏ **9.8(g) Enter *R*:\Source\Step 9 in the From directory field, where *R* is the drive letter of your CD-ROM drive, and press the Tab key.**

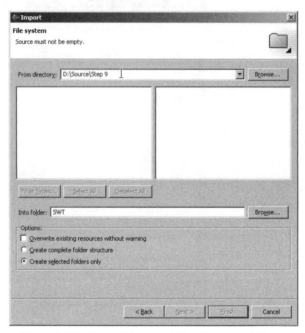

Figure 9.58: Enter R:\Source\Step 9, where R is the drive where you loaded the CD-ROM.

❏ **9.8(h) Left-click on the Step 9 folder.**

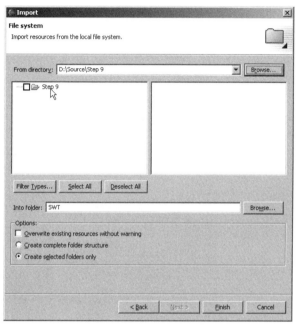

Figure 9.59: Select the Step 9 folder by left-clicking on it.

This will cause the contents of the Step 9 folder to appear in the right-hand pane, as shown in Figure 9.60.

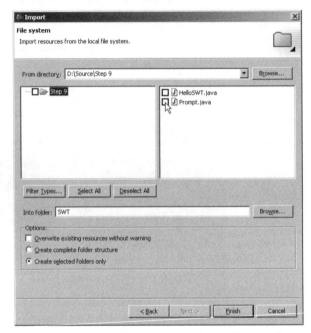

Figure 9.60: The contents of the Step 9 folder will appear in the right-hand pane.

Select Prompt.java by clicking on its checkbox.

❑ **9.8(i) Select Prompt.java and click Finish.**

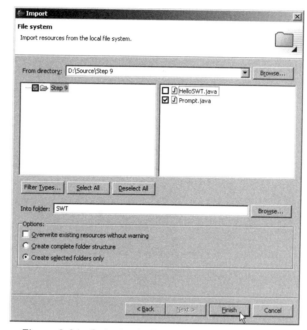

Figure 9.61: Select only Prompt.java, then click Finish.

If you also executed Option 1, you'll get the following dialog box. Click Yes and skip to Step 9.9.

❑ **9.8(j) Select Yes on the confirmation box that pops up.**

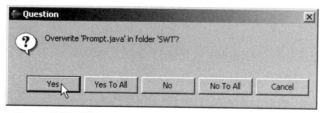

Figure 9.62: This prompt is used to be sure you really want to overwrite your source.

If you didn't execute Option 1, your display should look just like the one shown in Figure 9.63.

❑ 9.8(k) Open Prompt.java.

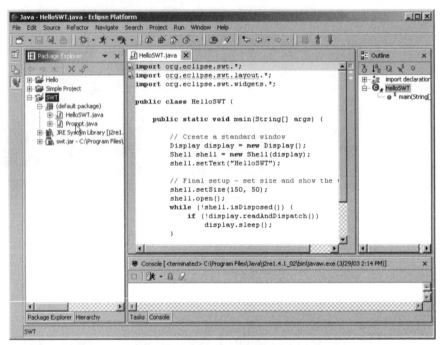

Figure 9.63: Open up the source for Prompt.java by double-clicking on it.

Your display should now look like Figure 9.64.

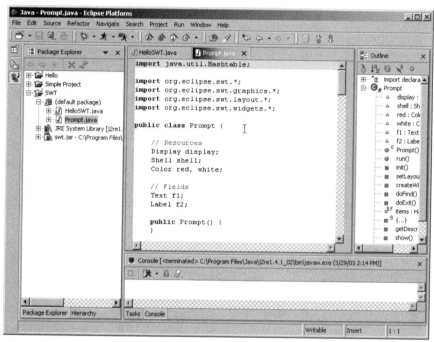

Figure 9.64: The source for Prompt.java.

Step 9.9—Running the Prompt class

GOAL

In this step you'll modify your
machine to run SWT applications more easily.

❏ **9.9(a) Select the Prompt class by left-clicking on it.**

❏ **9.9(b) From the Run tool dropdown, select Run As/Java Application.**

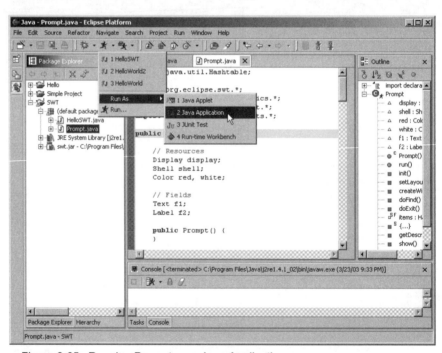

Figure 9.65: Running Prompt as a Java Application.

This will create a launch configuration for Prompt with the default characteristics
and then attempt to run it.

However, you'll run into the same problem you did with HelloSWT: The JVM won't be able to find the native implementation, as shown in Figure 9.66.

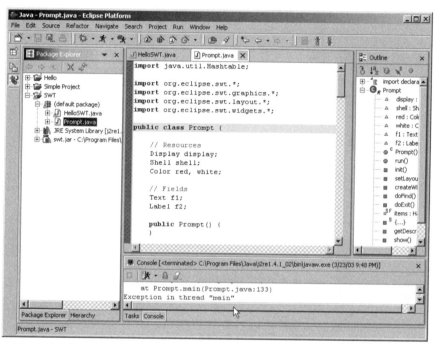

Figure 9.66: Red text once again indicates that you've got a problem.

❏ **9.9(c) Expand the error.**

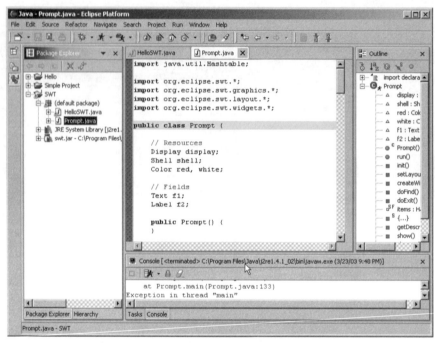

Figure 9.67: Expand the error by double-clicking on the Console view's title bar.

You'll see the error as shown in Figure 9.68.

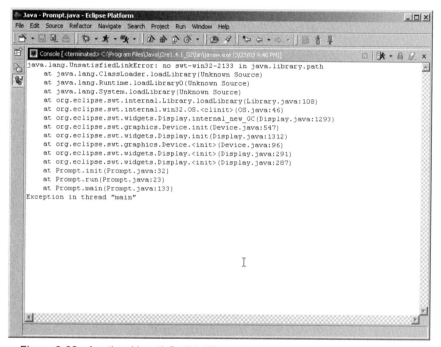

Figure 9.68: Another UnsatisfiedLinkError—in fact, the same one as in Step 9.6.

❑ 9.9(d) Restore the error to normal size.

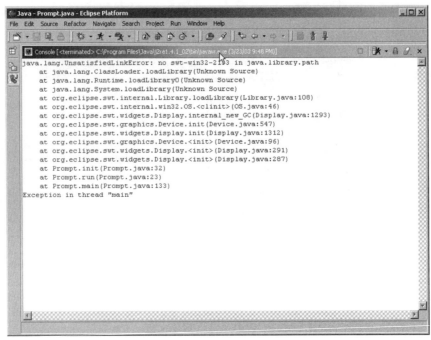

Figure 9.69: Restore the error to normal size by double-clicking on its title bar again.

Now you'll see the workbench as in Figure 9.70—back to normal size for the error, but an error still exists.

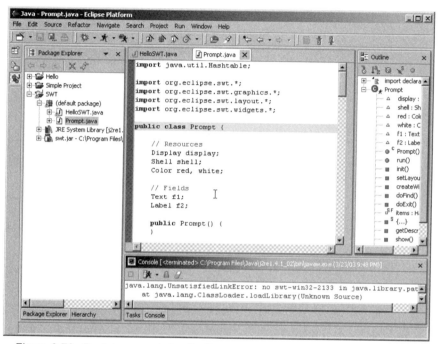

Figure 9.70: Back to normal size for the error.

You could just go in and change the launch configuration as you did with HelloSWT. This is a valid method, and it's the technique you should use for new library files until they are tested. However, I want to show you a different technique that you should use once you're comfortable that the library works.

Once again you'll use the command prompt.

❏ **9.9(e) Start a Windows command line and execute the following commands.**

You'll be using the value for $LIBPATH that you wrote down in Step 9.6(i).

```
Microsoft Windows 2000 [Version 5.00.2195]
(C) Copyright 1985-2000 Microsoft Corp.
Microsoft Windows 2000 [Version 5.00.2195]
(C) Copyright 1985-2000 Microsoft Corp.

C:\>echo %PATH%
C:\WINNT;C:\WINNT\System32;C:\WINNT\System32\Wbem

C:\>copy "c:\Program Files\eclipse\plugins\org.eclipse.swt.win32_2.1.0\os\win32\
86\*" c:\WINNT
c:\Program Files\eclipse\plugins\org.eclipse.swt.win32_2.1.0\os\win32\x86\swt-wi
n32-2133.dll
        1 file(s) copied.
```

1. echo %PATH%

   This will show you your path. You should see "C:\WINNT" in the path. If not, you have a very nonstandard Windows configuration, and I assume you're an expert and can modify the next step as appropriate.

2. copy "c:\Program Files\eclipse\plugins\org.eclipse.swt.win32_2.1.0\os\win32\x86*" c:\WINNT

   The format of this line is

   copy "$LIBPATH*" C:\WINNT

   This line copies the SWT native library from its Eclipse library into your system's library path. This will allow the system to find it. As I mentioned at the beginning of this step, the folder name is the $LIBPATH value you saved in Step 9.6(i).

> **Note:** Each time you upgrade Eclipse, you may have to repeat this step. If there are changes to the native libraries, the Eclipse team renames the library and changes all references to the new name. To see if this is necessary, try to run one of your simple SWT example applications. If you get the UnsatisfiedLinkError, you'll need to repeat this step.

Now go back and rerun the application.

❏ **9.9(f) Using the Run tool, re-run Prompt.**

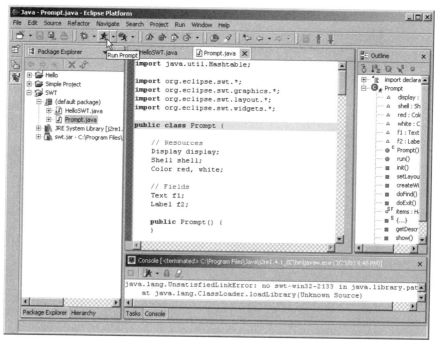

Figure 9.71: Running the application again.

This time you will get very different results, as shown on the next page.

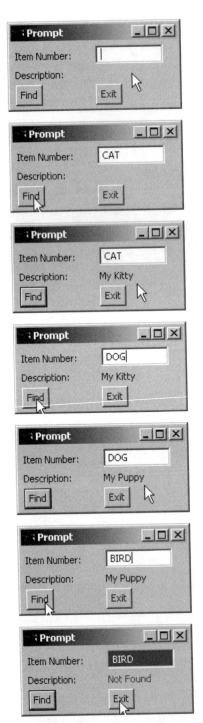

This is the result of the application. You can enter various values in the Item Number field and click the Find button to see if the value you entered is valid. If it is, you will see a description (the valid item numbers are CAT, DOG, and OCTOPUS). If you enter an invalid item number, the program will highlight the field as well as returning a value of Not Found.

You can run this as many times as you like. Select the Exit button when you want the application to end.

At this point, you can either finish up this step by reading the review of the code in the following pages, or you can just skip directly to the next step, Step 10, where you will attach a database to this program.

Code review: Prompt

Prompt is a simple application that is meant only to show a few things: how to use a layout in a window, how to add components to a layout, how to interact with components via listeners, and finally how to change the appearance of components. You'll also be introduced to a couple of simple concepts, such as resource disposal.

```
import java.util.Hashtable;

import org.eclipse.swt.*;
import org.eclipse.swt.graphics.*;
import org.eclipse.swt.layout.*;
import org.eclipse.swt.widgets.*;
```

The java.util.Hashtable import is hopefully self-explanatory, and the others are all standard imports in just about any SWT application.

- org eclipse.swt allows the use of the various SWT constants.

- org eclipse.swt.graphics allows the use of the Color class.

- org eclipse.swt.layout allows the use of the SWT layouts.

- org eclipse.swt.widgets defines most components and the like.

```
public class Prompt {
```

Prompt is a public class. Nothing special here.

```
// Resources
Display display;
Shell shell;
Color red, white;

// Fields
Text f1;
Label f2;
```

Here are some global resources for the class. I define the application resources (the Display, Shell and Color, most of which must be disposed of), as well as the application widgets f1 and f2-the ones that must be changed during the application. These are the fields whose attributes change in response to user input.

```
public Prompt() {
}
```

The constructor is very simple. I prefer to do a lazy initialization at run time.

```
public void run() {
        init();
        setLayout();
        createWidgets();
        show();
        cleanup();
}
```

This is the primary execution flow. The run method is invoked from main, and it executes individual subprocedures. Each subprocedure has its own specific tasks:

- init creates the Display and Shell objects as well as any global resources.

- setLayout applies the appropriate layout object to the window.

- createWidgets creates the actual user interface widgets such as buttons and fields, including associating the listeners.

- show executes the dispatch loop.

- cleanup disposes of all resources.

```
private void init() {
        // Create a standard window
        display = new Display();
        shell = new Shell(display);
        shell.setText("Prompt3");
        // Create some colors
        red = new Color(display, 255, 0, 0);
        white = new Color(display, 255, 255, 255);
}
```

The init method is used to create the Display and Shell objects for the primary window, as well as create the Color objects that are used in other methods.

```
private void setLayout() {
        // Create the layout for the widgets
        GridLayout grid = new GridLayout();
        grid.numColumns = 2;
        grid.makeColumnsEqualWidth = true;
        shell.setLayout(grid);
}
```

The setLayout method creates a GridLayout object with two columns. Each row in the layout holds exactly two widgets. The first two rows contain a label and a field, and the last row contains two buttons. For more complex windows, you can nest grids inside one another or use other layout classes.

The createWidgets method is the most complex method. It creates each of the individual user interface (UI) components, and for some of them it adds listeners.

```java
private void createWidgets() {
    // Create my widgets
    Label l1 = new Label(shell, SWT.NONE);
    l1.setText("Item Number:");

    f1 = new Text(shell, SWT.BORDER | SWT.SINGLE);
    f1.setTextLimit(20);

    Label l2 = new Label(shell, SWT.NONE);
    l2.setText("Description:");

    f2 = new Label(shell, SWT.NONE);
    f2.setText(" ");
```

These are the simple UI components, the labels and fields. The user interacts with them to a small degree, but the application doesn't really handle individual events for these fields. It lets the system handle the events.

```java
    Button b1 = new Button(shell, SWT.PUSH);
    b1.setText("Find");
    b1.addListener(SWT.Selection, new Listener() {
        public void handleEvent(Event event) {
            doFind();
        }
    });

    Button b2 = new Button(shell, SWT.PUSH);
    b2.setText("Exit");
    b2.addListener(SWT.Selection, new Listener() {
        public void handleEvent(Event event) {
            doExit();
        }
    });
}
```

Buttons, on the other hand, usually require application attention. They are the way the user tells the application to do something. In this case, each button is attached to a Listener object. Listeners are special objects designed to handle events. In this very simple design, each listener simply passes the event directly to another method. I use this convention often, where the name of the method is "do" followed by the button name. In this application, the two buttons are Find and Exit, so the two button listener methods are doFind and doExit.

```
private void doFind() {
    String desc = getDescription(f1.getText());
    if (desc == null)
    {
        f1.setForeground(white);
        f1.setBackground(red);
        f2.setText("Not Found");
        f2.setForeground(red);
    }
    else
    {
        f1.setForeground(null);
        f1.setBackground(null);
        f2.setText(desc);
        f2.setForeground(null);
    }
}
```

The doFind method is actually the only "business logic" in the application. It passes the item number entered by the user, (f1.getText()), to the getDescription method. If a null value is returned, then the item number was not found, and the appropriate error actions are taken: The description is set to not found, and both the input field and description are changed to a red background or foreground to indicate an error condition. Otherwise the value is assumed to be good, and the fields are set back to their default colors.

```
private void doExit() {
        shell.close();
}
```

The doExit method is one of the simplest methods. It only has to invoke the close method of the shell object, which will in turn cause the event loop to end.

```
private static final Hashtable items;
static {
        items = new Hashtable();
        items.put("DOG", "My Puppy");
        items.put("CAT", "My Kitty");
        items.put("OCTOPUS", "Calamari Kid");
}
```

This is a special static variable that has its own static initializer. The first time this class is accessed, this routine is invoked and the Hashtable named items is filled with a few hardcoded values.

```
private String getDescription(String item)
{
        return (String) items.get(item);
}
```

This method simulates a database inquiry by looking for the item number passed into it in the items table.

```
private void show() {
        // Final setup - size the display show it
        shell.setSize(200, 100);
        shell.open();
        while (!shell.isDisposed()) {
                if (!display.readAndDispatch())
                        display.sleep();
        }
}
```

The show method is pretty standard (except maybe for hardcoding the size of the window). Basically, it just opens the window then begins the event-dispatching loop. When the window is closed, the method returns.

```
private void cleanup() {
    // When done, clean up resources
    display.dispose();
    red.dispose();
    white.dispose();
}
```

This method is invoked at the end of the application, and it is used to dispose of any resources that were allocated during the application. This should be a standard method for any application that allocates resources.

```
public static void main(String[] args) {
    new Prompt().run();
    System.exit(0);
}
}
```

This is a slight twist on the old main method. In this case, the main method does nothing more than create a new Prompt object and execute its run method. Upon completion, the main method then exits. This is a very clean programming style.

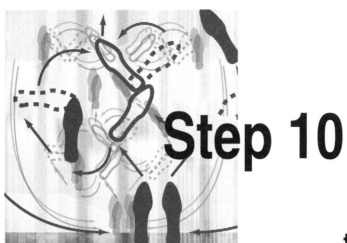

Step 10

Adding
the database

Step 9 introduced you to a Java user interface. You used the SWT classes to create and deploy a simple application. Now it's time to connect that application to a database. Step 10 is all about the data.

Overview

In the steps that led to this point, you've become accustomed to the Eclipse workbench and you've created a simple user interface. The last step in the journey is to attach that user interface to a back-end database.

I'll be using JDBC for this. Unfortunately, due to the limitations of most of the available SQL databases, I'll only be able to use the original JDBC syntax (sometimes called JDBC1). I suggest, however, if you haven't already done so, that you take the time to learn about JDBC2 and JDBC3. JDBC2 in particular, with scrollable and updatable result sets, goes a long way towards making JDBC functional in a business application.

You may have your own SQL database available. For example, you may have access to an Oracle SQL engine or a Microsoft Sequel Server. Or you might be running MySQL on your workstation, or any one of a number of other workstation-based SQL engines. Or you might be using IBM's Java Toolkit to access the database on an IBM iSeries.

If you have your own JDBC-capable database, then you simply need to know the following pieces of information:

1. The name of the driver class

2. The name and location of the JAR file containing the driver

3. The URL used to access the database

4. The user ID and password

You must have the authority to add and delete tables in the database. If all of these conditions have been met, you can proceed directly to Step 10.2.

Otherwise, Step 10.1 will guide you through installing HSQLDB, the free open-source SQL engine from SourceForge. HSQLDB is 100% Pure Java and is very easy to get started with. It doesn't currently support JDBC2, but it's perfectly adequate for learning purposes.

For more information on other SQL databases, please see SideStep 5.

Step 10.1—Installing HSQLDB

GOAL

**In this step, you will install
HSQLDB from the accompanying CD.**

Note: HSQLDB is an Open Source project. Releases are very irregular, but development seems to be continuing. The version included on the CD-ROM (version 1.7.1) has been thoroughly tested with these programs. You can always get the latest version from hsqldb.sourceforge.net, but obviously I can't guarantee that it will work with this code. Feel free, though, to play with newer versions if you feel adventurous. Once you download the ZIP file, open the downloaded version in WinZip, then proceed to Step 10.1(f).

Note: If you are using an extraction tool other than WinZip, then use that tool to extract the files from the ZIP file into C:\Program Files\SQL. Be sure to use folder names when extracting the files. Once the files have been extracted, you may continue directly to Step 10.2.

If you are using WinZip to extract and install the included software, follow these steps.

☐ **10.1(a) Insert the CD-ROM included with this book into your CD-ROM drive.**

☐ **10.1(b) Start WinZip.**

At this point, if the "Tip of the Day" comes up, close it.

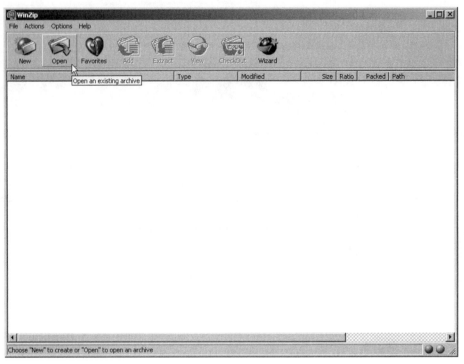

Figure 10.1: The WinZip main screen.

❏ **10.1(c) Double-click on the Software folder.**

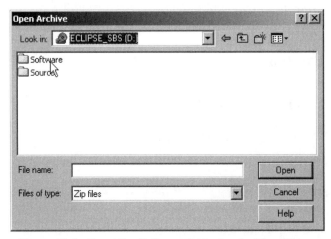

Figure 10.2: Open the Software folder by double-clicking.

❑ **10.1(d) Double-click on the HSQLDB folder.**

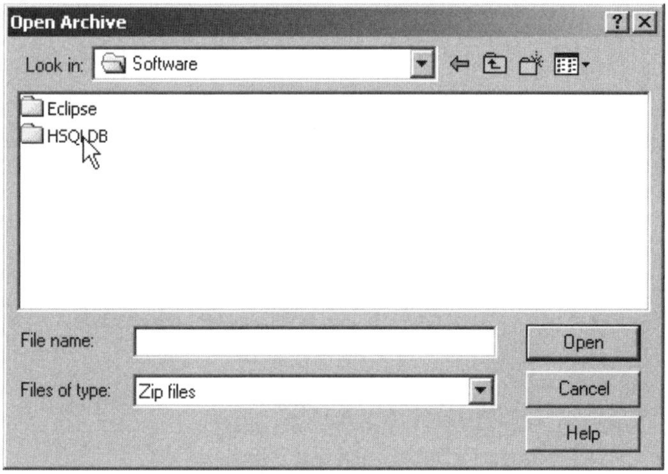

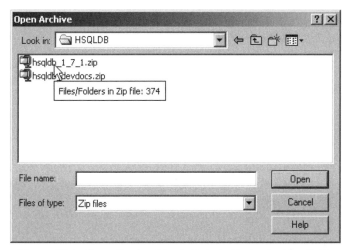

Figure 10.3: Open the HSQLDB folder by double-clicking.

❑ **10.1(e) Double-click on the file hsqldb_1_7_1.zip.**

I've also included a file hsqldb_devdocs.zip, which contains documentation. It's not necessary at this time to open that file. You can extract the documentation some other time as you see fit.

Figure 10.4: Open the hsqldb_1_7_1.zip file by double-clicking.

Double-clicking hsqldb_1_7_1.zip will return you to a display of the contents of the hsqldb_1_7_1.zip file, as shown in Figure 10.5.

❑ **10.1(f)   Click the Extract button.**

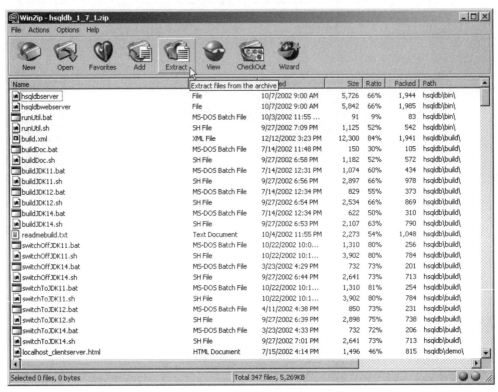

Figure 10.5: Click the Extract button to begin the extraction process.

❑ **10.1(g) In the Extract to: field, type 'C:\Program Files\SQL'.**

❑ **10.1(h) Be sure 'Use folder names' is checked, and click Extract.**

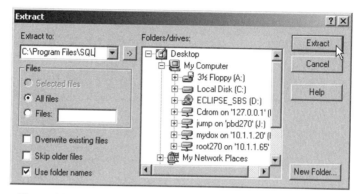

Figure 10.6: Select folder C:\Program Files\SQL and press Extract.

You'll see a window like the one in Figure 10.7 while the tool extracts the files.

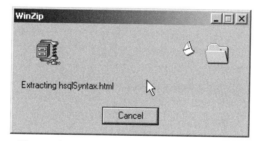

Figure 10.7: The extraction status display.

When the extraction is finished, the status window will disappear, and you'll be returned to the primary WinZip window, as in Figure 10.8.

❑ **10.1(i)   Close the WinZip tool.**

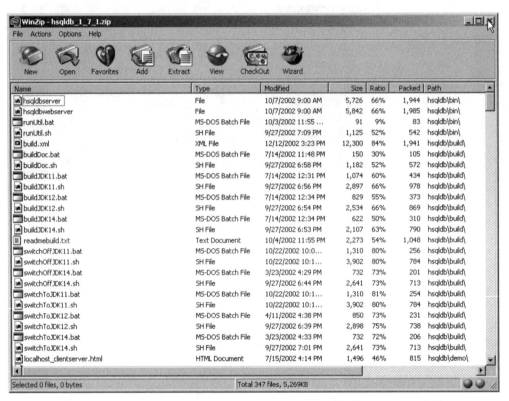

Figure 10.8: Close WinZip using the X (or you could use the File/Exit menu option).

Step 10.2—Add a new class, HelloHSQL

Note: At this point, you can either add a new class and type in the code, or import the class directly from the included CD-ROM. If you would like more practice with the editor, then continue with Steps 10.2 and 10.3. If you would rather just import the code and move on to testing, then skip ahead to Step 10.4.

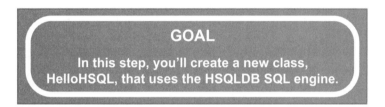

GOAL

In this step, you'll create a new class, HelloHSQL, that uses the HSQLDB SQL engine.

❑ **10.2(a) Make sure the SWT project is selected.**

❑ **10.2(b) Right click in the Package Explorer, select New/Class.**

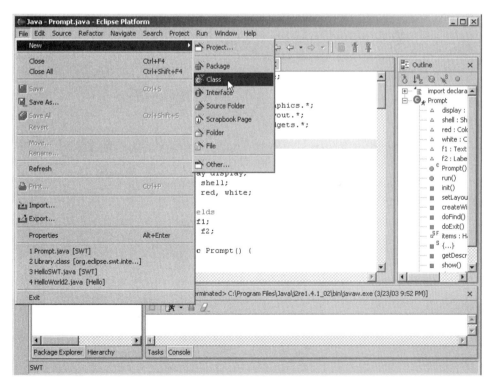

Figure 10.9: Creating a new class using the New/Class menu option.

❑ **10.2(c) Make sure the Source Folder is 'SWT'.**

❑ **10.2(d) Leave Package blank.**

❑ **10.2(e) Leave Enclosing type unchecked.**

❑ **10.2(f) Enter 'HelloHSQL' in the Name field.**

❑ **10.2(g) Make sure public is checked, abstract and final are unchecked.**

❑ **10.2(h) Leave Superclass as java.lang.Object, Interfaces blank.**

❑ **10.2(i) Make sure public static void main(String[] args) is checked.**

❑ **10.2(j) Leave Constructors from superclass and Inherited abstract methods unchecked.**

❑ **10.2(k) Click Finish.**

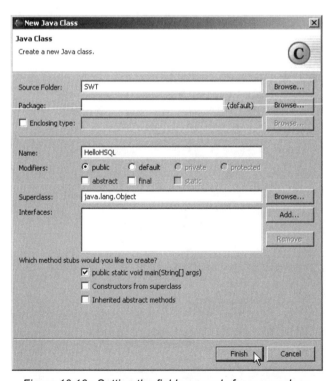

Figure 10.10: Setting the fields properly for a new class.

This will create a public class HelloHSQL in the default package (because you left Package blank) in project SWT. In Steps 10.2(i) and 10.2(j) you instructed the IDE to create a standard "main" method but no other methods. That being the case, you will see the result as in Figure 10.11.

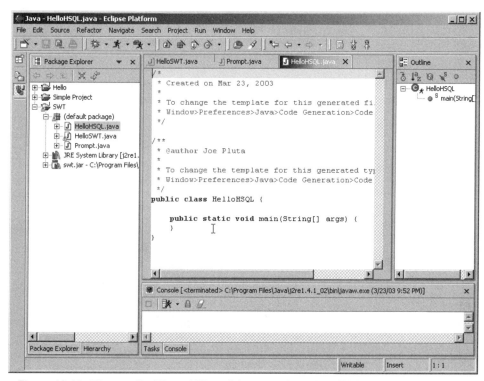

Figure 10.11: The result of the addition of the new class HelloSWT.

Step 10.3—Write the code for the HelloHSQL class

GOAL

In this step you'll enter a
simple JDBC application that will use
HSQLDB to load some data into a table.

❑ **10.3(a) Enter the source code below after the comments.**

```java
import java.sql.*;

public class HelloHSQL {

    private static final String SQLCLASS = "org.hsqldb.jdbcDriver";
    private static final String SQLURL   = "jdbc:hsqldb:hsqldb";
    private static final String SQLUSER  = "sa";
    private static final String SQLPWD   = "";

    public static void main(String[] args) {

        try {
            // Create a connection
            Class.forName (SQLCLASS);
            Connection c = DriverManager.getConnection(SQLURL, SQLUSER, SQLPWD);
            Statement s = c.createStatement();

            // Delete and recreate the table
            try {
                s.execute("DROP TABLE ITEMS");
            } catch (Exception e) {}
            s.execute("CREATE TABLE ITEMS (ItemNumber CHAR, Description CHAR)");

            // Insert data
            s.execute("INSERT INTO ITEMS VALUES ('DOG', 'Cuddly Duddly')");
            s.execute("INSERT INTO ITEMS VALUES ('CAT', 'Felix the Cat')");
            s.execute("INSERT INTO ITEMS VALUES ('OCTOPUS', 'Squidworth')");

            // Check the results
            ResultSet rs = s.executeQuery("SELECT * FROM ITEMS");
            while (rs.next())
            {
                System.out.println(
                "Item: " + rs.getString("ItemNumber") +
```

```
            ", Description: " + rs.getString("Description"));
            }

            // Shut down
            s.close();
            c.close();

        } catch (Exception e) {
            System.out.println("Error: " + e);
        }

        // When done, clean up resource and exit
        System.exit(0);
    }
}
```

At this point, your screen will look like the one in Figure 10.12.

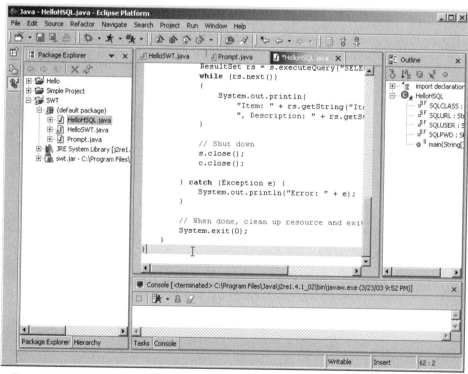

Figure 10.12: Source code entered into the editor pane.

Use the scroll bar to reposition the source window to the top of the code. You can also use standard editing keystrokes, such as Ctrl-Home.

❑ **10.3(b) Position window to top of source.**

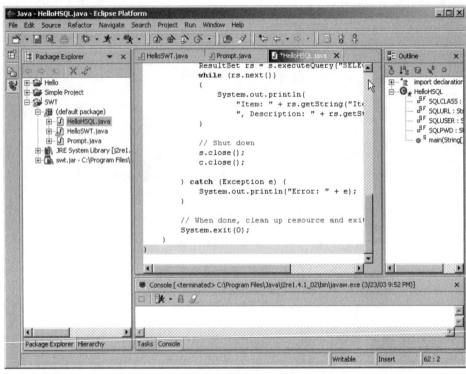

Figure 10.13: Using the scroll bar to position the window to the top of the source.

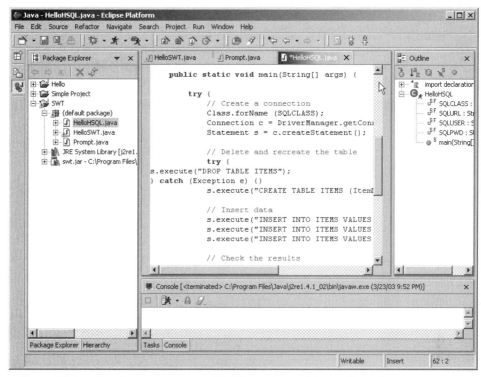

Figure 10.14: It's a larger source, so you'll have to scroll two or three times.

Now save the source. You can use the Save tool on the main Eclipse tool bar, Ctrl-S, or the editor popup menu. I'll use the Save tool:

❑ **10.3(c) Click on the Save icon on the tool bar.**

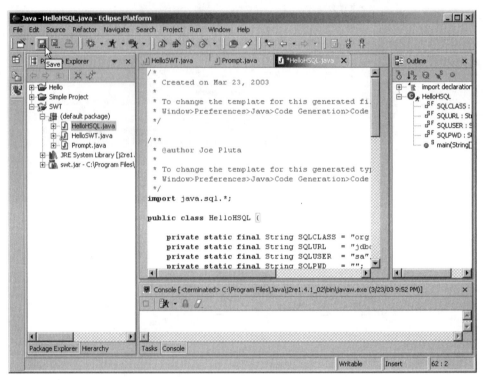

Figure 10.15: Using the Save tool to save the source.

You'll see the screen shown in Figure 10.16. You may skip ahead now to Step 10.5.

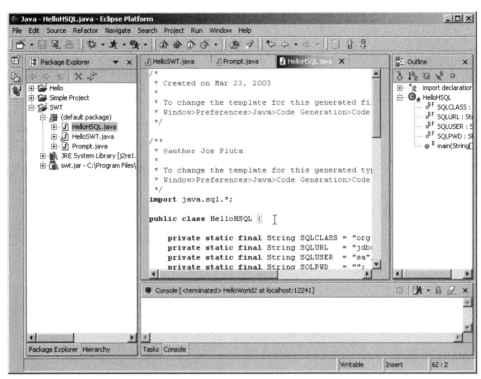

Figure 10.16: The workbench after saving the new HelloHSQL source.

Step 10.4—Import the HelloHSQL application

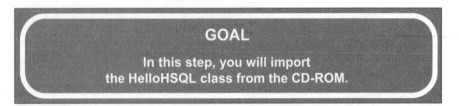

GOAL

In this step, you will import
the HelloHSQL class from the CD-ROM.

❑ **10.4(a)   Insert the CD-ROM included with this book into your CD-ROM drive.**

❑ **10.4(b)   Right click on the SWT project and select Import . . .**

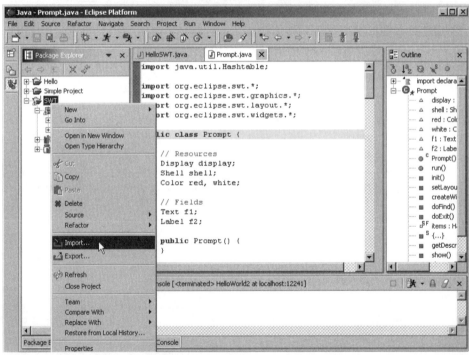

Figure 10.17: Use the popup menu in the Package Explorer to Import a file into the SWT project.

At this point, you have many options as to your import source. Since your source is in a folder on the CD-ROM disk, you'll use the File System option.

❑ **10.4(c) Select File System and click Next.**

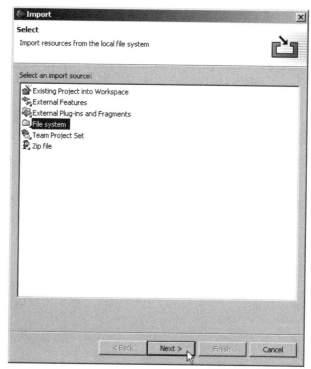

Figure 10.18: Select File System as the source for the import.

You need to specify the location of the files. Specify *R*:\Source\Step 10, where *R* is the letter of the CD-ROM drive where you loaded the disk. Remember from Step 7 that on my machine the CD is loaded in the D: drive, so I replace *R* with D in the From directory: field as shown in Figure 10.19.

❑ **10.4(d) Enter *R*:\Source\Step 10 in the Directory field, where *R* is the drive letter of your CD-ROM drive, and press the Tab key.**

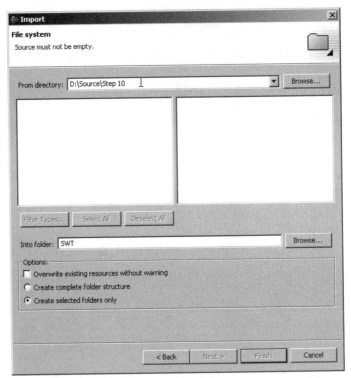

Figure 10.19: Enter R:\Source\Step 10, where R is the drive where you loaded the included CD-ROM.

The Tab key will cause the left pane to be loaded with an icon for the Step 10 folder. Select the Step 10 folder by clicking on it.

❏ **10.4(e) Left-click on the Step 10 folder.**

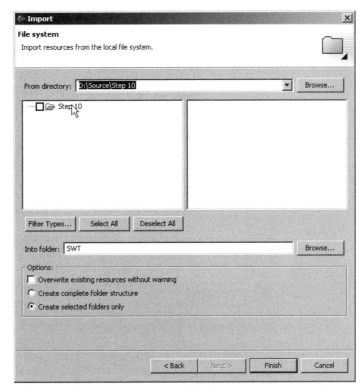

Figure 10.20: Select the Step 10 folder by left-clicking on it.

This will cause the contents of the Step 10 folder to appear in the right-hand pane as shown in Figure 10.21.

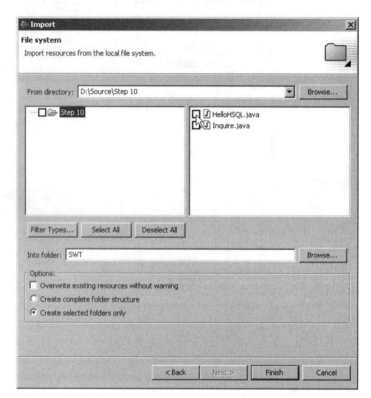

Figure 10.21: The contents of the Step 10 folder will appear in the right hand pane.

Select HelloHSQL.java by clicking on its checkbox. Don't worry about Inquire.java; you'll get to that in a later step.

❑ **10.4(f) Select HelloHSQL.java and click Finish.**

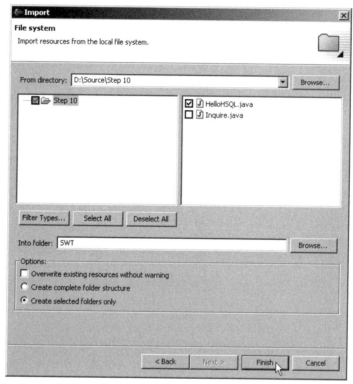

Figure 10.22: Select only HelloHSQL.java, then press Finish.

Your display should look just like the one shown in Figure 10.23.

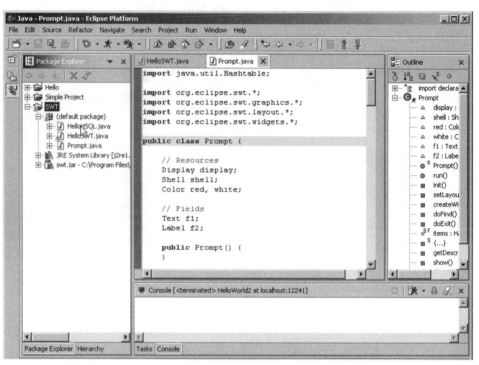

Figure 10.23: The workbench display after importing my source code.

Notice that the HelloHSQL class has been added, but that you don't see its source. The editor will not automatically open a source member that has been imported. You must do that manually.

❏ 10.4(g) Open HelloHSQL.java by double-clicking on it.

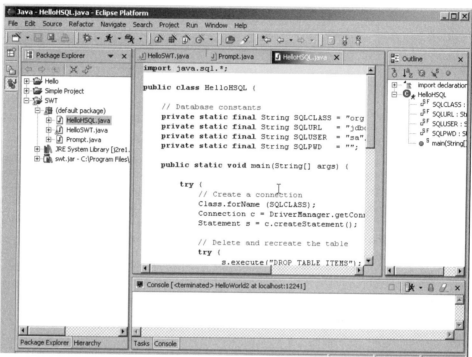

Figure 10.24: The imported version of HelloHSQL (you can tell by the lack of opening comments).

Step 10.5—Modifying the JDBC constants (EXPERT ONLY!)

GOAL

In this step, you will modify, if necessary, the JDBC constants that allow you to attach to your SQL database.

Note: If you intend to use the HSQLDB database that was included on the CD-ROM (or if you downloaded HSQLDB yourself), then the constants are all set correctly, and you can continue directly to Step 10.6.

If you have your own SQL database and are a skilled JDBC programmer, you can modify this program to use your database. Do not attempt this unless you have already written JDBC programs.

The following code initializes the four JDBC constants:

```
private static final String SQLCLASS = "org.hsqldb.jdbcDriver";
private static final String SQLURL   = "jdbc:hsqldb:hsqldb";
private static final String SQLUSER  = "sa";
private static final String SQLPWD   = "";
```

The SQLCLASS field defines the name of the driver. This really identifies the database provider, such as Oracle or PostGreSQL. In this case, org.hsqldb.jdbcDriver is the name of the HSQLDB driver.

The SQLURL field identifies the specific database you are connecting to (such as test or production). The format of this field depends on the database provider. For HSQLDB, the syntax shown says to use a database named "hsqldb" located in the current working directory.

Finally, the SQLUSER and SQLPWD fields identify the user ID and password that will be used to access the database. For this example, user "sa" is a special user (system administrator), that tells HSQLDB to create the database from scratch if it doesn't exist.

If you change these values, be sure you know what to change them to. A change here will also change which JAR file must be added in Step 10.6. I have included some example configurations for other databases in SideStep 5.

Step 10.6—Running the HelloHSQL class

GOAL

In this step you will try to run the class you just created.

Run the class from the Run menu of the Eclipse main menu bar.

☐ **10.6(a) Select the HelloHSQL class by left-clicking on it.**

☐ **10.6(b) From the Run tool, select Run As/Java Application.**

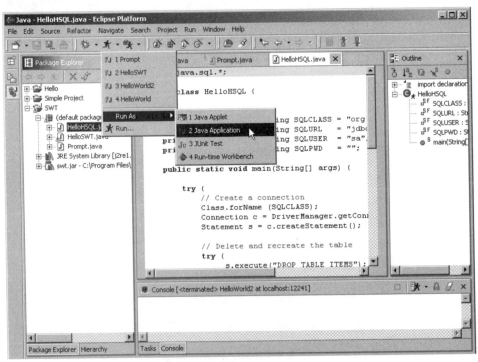

Figure 10.25: Running HelloHSQL as a Java Application.

This will create a launch configuration for HelloHSQL with the default characteristics and then attempt to run it.

Once again, you won't meet with a lot of success, as you can see in Figure 10.26. And even though the console view is rather small, the error is pretty compact and very concise: ClassNotFoundException: org.hsqldb.jdbcDriver.

This is actually a very common error during JDBC programming, and it just means that you haven't yet added the SQL engine's JAR file to your classpath, which you can do immediately.

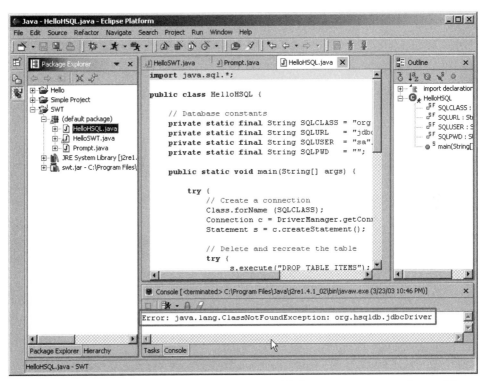

Figure 10.26: Blue text is system console output—this is your own error routine and it shows that you're missing HSQLDB's JAR file.

❏ **10.6(c) Right-click on the SWT Project.**

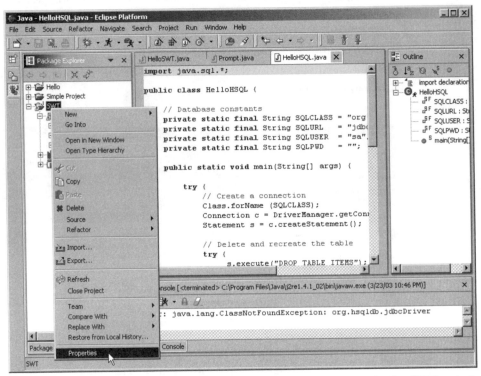

Figure 10.27: Using the popup menu to access the properties dialog for the SWT project.

The classpath is on the Java Build Path properties sheet, under the Libraries tab. You should already be there, but if not:

❏ **10.6(d) Select the Java Build Path properties sheet.**

❏ **10.6(e) Select the Libraries tab.**

Add the JAR file by using the Add External JARs button.

❑ **10.6(f) Click 'Add External JARs . . .'**

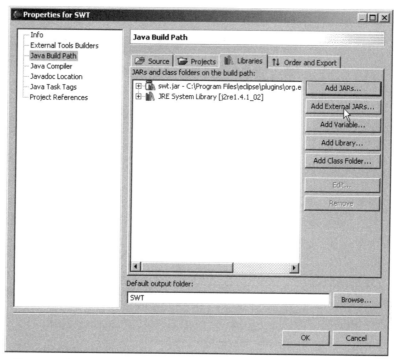

Figure 10.28: Click Add External JARs . . .

A standard file finder dialog will appear. It will probably be in the win32 folder; that's the last folder you imported a JAR file from.

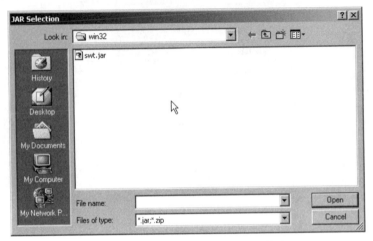

Figure 10.29: The last folder you added a JAR file from.

Navigate to where you installed HSQLDB in Step 10.1.

Note: If you're using a database other than HSQLDB, you will need to include your own JAR file in these next steps.

❏ **10.6(g) Type 'C:\Program Files\SQL' into the File name field and click Open.**

Figure 10.30: Open the SQL folder where you installed HSQLDB back in Step 10.1.

Next, open the HSQLDB folder (which should be named hsqldb).

❏ **10.6(h) Open the folder named hsqldb.**

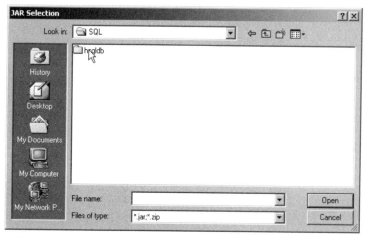

Figure 10.31: Open the hsqldb folder.

❑ **10.6(i)   Open the folder named lib.**

Figure 10.32: Open the lib folder.

Now you will have reached a point where you see a JAR file named hsqldb.jar. This is the JAR file that you want to include on your classpath.

❑ **10.6(j)   Open the file named hsqldb.jar.**

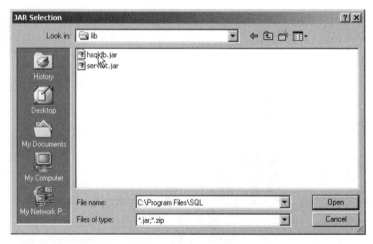

Figure 10.33: Open hsqldb.jar, which includes it in the classpath.

You'll see that the JAR file has been added to the Libraries tab. Just click OK to continue.

❑ **10.6(k) Click OK.**

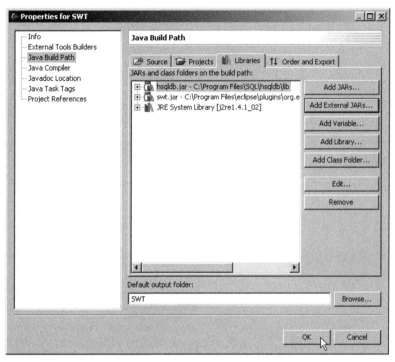

Figure 10.34: The new JAR file is in the Libraries tab, so press OK.

Your workbench should now look like the one in Figure 10.35. Interestingly, there are still some warning messages. But if you'll look closely, you'll see that while you got rid of all the errors for HelloHSQL, the old warnings for HelloSWT popped up again. This could be a little confusing, so always watch this list carefully.

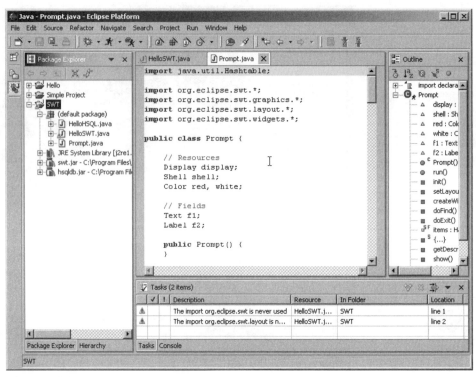

Figure 10.35: No errors.

❑ **10.6(l)   Click the Run tool to rerun HelloHSQL.**

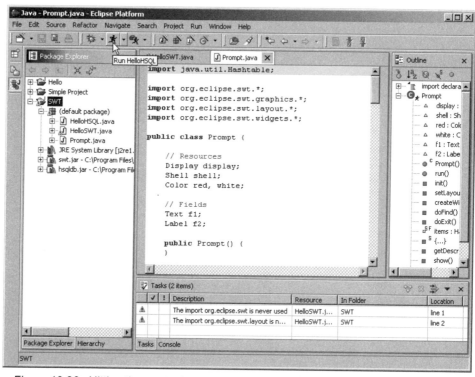

Figure 10.36: Hitting the run tool reruns the last application, which in this case is HelloHSQL.

You will see the screen below. Notice that records for DOG, CAT, and OCTOPUS have all been entered. Congratulations!

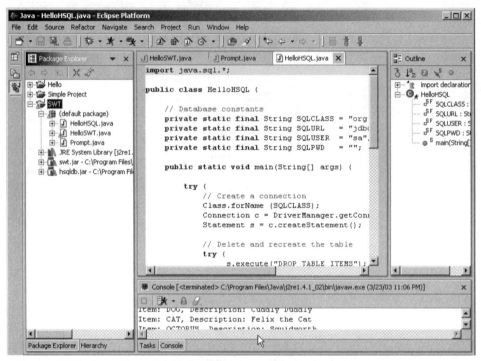

Figure 10.37: Output from the HelloHSQL class.

Code review: HelloHSQL

```
import java.sql.*;
```

This is the standard import command for JDBC programs; it defines the primary JDBC classes such as Driver, Connection, and Statement.

```
public class HelloHSQL {
```

This is standard code for any runnable Java application.

```
private static final String SQLCLASS = "org.hsqldb.jdbcDriver";
private static final String SQLURL   = "jdbc:hsqldb:hsqldb";
private static final String SQLUSER  = "sa";
private static final String SQLPWD   = "";
```

These are the JDBC constants. I go into them in some detail in Step 10.5. In general, the class and URL are determined by the SQL engine vendor, while the user ID and password are up to you. In this particular case, however, the user ID "sa" is a special user ID for the HSQLDB product—it will initialize the database if it does not already exist. So please don't change this code unless you're very comfortable with what you're doing.

```
public static void main(String[] args) {
```

More standard Java application code.

```
try {
```

Note that all of the SQL code is inside a try/catch block. This is the standard Java technique for checking for errors in called methods. The called method will "throw" an exception, and the calling method will "catch" it. This technique is very powerful, but it can sometimes lead to complicated code (an example of which I'll show you in a moment). This particular try block, however, is pretty straightforward—it encompasses all the code in the main method; the catch is at the bottom of the code.

```
// Create a connection
Class.forName (SQLCLASS);
Connection c = DriverManager.getConnection(SQLURL, SQLUSER, SQLPWD);
Statement s = c.createStatement();
```

This code is very standard, although it's not exactly intuitive. The Class.forName() call causes a static initializer to be invoked, which registers the driver. For my tastes, this is a "clever" technique, and "clever" is not a compliment. In programming, "clever" code usually indicates code that is nonintuitive and may be easy to misunderstand. The only saving grace is that every JDBC vendor does this, so once you learn this particular technique, you'll find that it applies to every JDBC a pplication.

After that, the code simply creates a Connection, which represents a communication session with the host, and a Statement, which is used to execute SQL requests and return result sets when appropriate.

Up until this point, the code for every JDBC application is the same, or at least similar. There may be some minor differences as to runtime attributes or perhaps some slightly different code to take advantage of connection pooling, but in general, the idea is always the same: Instantiate the driver, open the connection, create a statement.

```
// Delete and recreate the table
try {
        s.execute("DROP TABLE ITEMS");
} catch (Exception e) {}
s.execute("CREATE TABLE ITEMS (ItemNumber CHAR, Description CHAR)");
```

This is the start of the application-specific code. The DROP command is used to delete an SQL table, while CREATE builds a new one. This is pretty low-level code, and wouldn't normally be part of a day-to-day application, but since you're starting from scratch, you're going to have to create the table sometime, and you may as well do it in a program—this tests that you have everything installed properly.

Take a close look at the line that executes the DROP command. You'll notice that there is a try/catch block around it. That's because the DROP is going to fail the first time you run this program (the table won't exist yet!), and the primary way that JDBC reports errors back to the user for these types of commands is through exceptions. Since the code is already inside a try/catch block, the not-found error would cause the program to end. So instead, I've put a nested try/catch block around just the DROP command. In this block, I ignore any errors. In a production application I would only catch for SQLException and verify that the error is "Table Not Found". If it wasn't, I'd throw the error to the higher level try/catch.

```
// Insert data
s.execute("INSERT INTO ITEMS VALUES ('DOG', 'Cuddly Duddly')");
s.execute("INSERT INTO ITEMS VALUES ('CAT', 'Felix the Cat')");
s.execute("INSERT INTO ITEMS VALUES ('OCTOPUS', 'Squidworth')");
```

These statements populate the table using the standard JDBC1 syntax. In JDBC1, all commands other than the SELECT statement are run using the execute method. JDBC2, on the other hand, allows more traditional record-based access, where you can position yourself in a file, update fields and then rewrite a record.

HSQLDB doesn't support the more powerful JDBC2 syntax. If you look through the SideStep, however, you'll find some examples of code that does take advantage of JDBC2. The SAPDB and the JTOpen drivers both support JDBC2.

```
// Check the results
ResultSet rs = s.executeQuery("SELECT * FROM ITEMS");
while (rs.next())
{
        System.out.println(
              "Item: " + rs.getString("ItemNumber") +
              ", Description: " + rs.getString("Description"));
}
```

This is a standard JDBC read loop. In JDBC, you create a ResultSet, which represents a set of rows in a specified order. The "next" method moves to the next record in the set, and returns false if there are no more. The getString method allows you to retrieve the value of a field as an object of type String. There are other methods available to get numeric data and so on, but the general idea is still the same: get the next row, extract out the columns using get*Xxx* methods, and loop until done.

```
// Shut down
s.close();
c.close();
```

At the end of the day, you need to clean up. This is especially important in distributed systems; not performing the appropriate shutdown steps can leave connections open and waste resources on the host. Always close your statement and your connection.

(In fact, you should probably use a finally clause in your try/catch block to shut down the connection if anything goes wrong, but that's a little bit outside the scope of this particular program.)

```
} catch (Exception e) {
     System.out.println("Error: " + e);
}
```

Here's the standard catch block. I'm not doing anything fancy—I just print the error message.

```
         // When done, clean up resource and exit
         System.exit(0);
     }
}
```

And finally, good Java programming practices dictate that an application always ends with System.exit(0). That's it for this program.

Step 10.7—Import the Inquire application

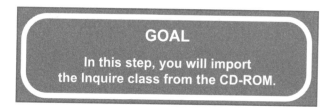

GOAL

In this step, you will import
the Inquire class from the CD-ROM.

☐ **10.7(a) Insert the CD-ROM included with this book into your CD-ROM drive.**

☐ **10.7(b) Right click on the SWT project and select Import . . .**

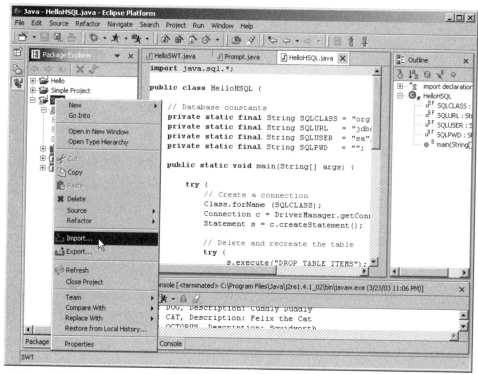

Figure 10.38: Use the popup menu in the Package Explorer to Import a file into the SWT project.

At this point, you have many options as to your import source. Since your source is in a folder on the CD-ROM disk, you'll use the File System option.

❑ **10.7(c) Select File System and click Next.**

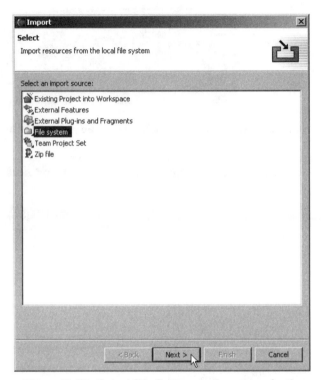

Figure 10.39: Select File System as the source for the import.

You need to specify the location of the files. Use the dropdown list for the "From directory" field to reselect the Step 10 folder. (If you don't see Step 10 in the dropdown, simply enter R:\Source\Step 10, where R is the letter of the CD-ROM drive where you loaded the disk, into the "From directory:" field and press the Tab key). Remember from Step 7 that on my machine the CD is loaded in the D: drive, so I enter D in place of R.

❏ **10.7(d) Use the dropdown list to reselect the Step 10 folder.**

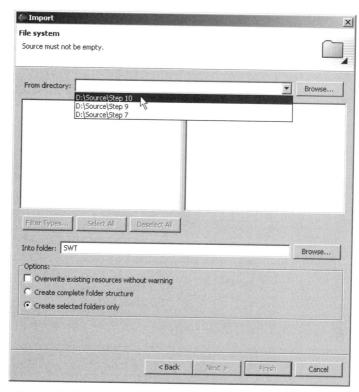

Figure 10.40: Enter R:\Source\Step 10, where R is the drive where you loaded the included CD-ROM.

Select the Step 10 folder by clicking on it.

❑ **10.7(e) Left-click on the Step 10 folder.**

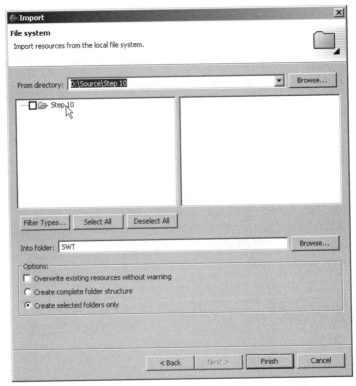

Figure 10.41: Select the Step 10 folder by left-clicking on it.

This will cause the contents of the Step 10 folder to appear in the right-hand pane as shown in Figure 10.42.

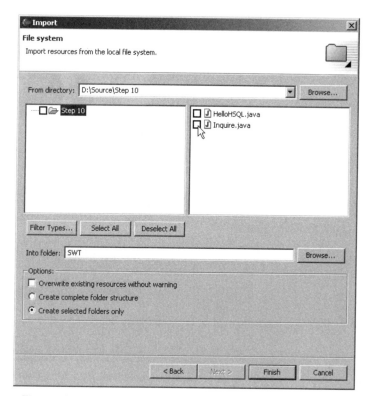

Figure 10.42: The contents of the Source folder will appear in the right hand pane.

Select Inquire.java by clicking on its checkbox.

❑ **10.7(f)   Select Inquire.java and click Finish.**

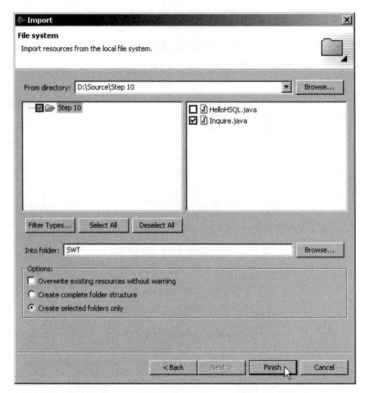

Figure 10.43: Select only Inquire.java, then click Finish.

Your display should look just like the one shown in Figure 10.44. Double-click on Inquire.java to open it.

❑ **10.7(g) Open Inquire.java by double-clicking on it.**

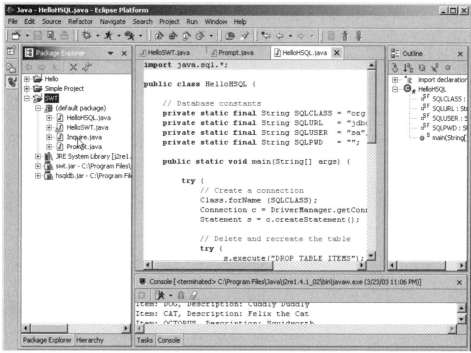

Figure 10.44: The workbench display after importing Inquire.java, but before opening it.

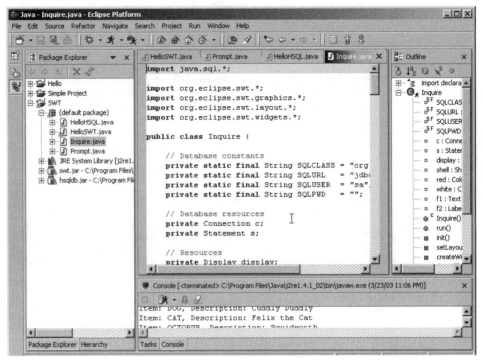

Figure 10.45: The workbench display after opening Inquire.java.

Step 10.8—Modifying the JDBC constants (EXPERT ONLY!)

> ## GOAL
>
> In this step, you will modify,
> if necessary, the JDBC constants that
> allow you to attach to your SQL database.

You will only change things in this step if you did so in the Step 10.5. If you made modifications to HelloHSQL.java in Step 10.5, please make the same modifications to Inquire.java here.

Step 10.9—Running the Inquire class

GOAL

In this step you will try
to run the class you just created.

Run the class from the Run menu of the Eclipse main menu bar.

☐ **10.9(a)   Select the Inquire class by left-clicking on it.**

☐ **10.9(b)   From the main menu bar, select Run/Run As/Java Application.**

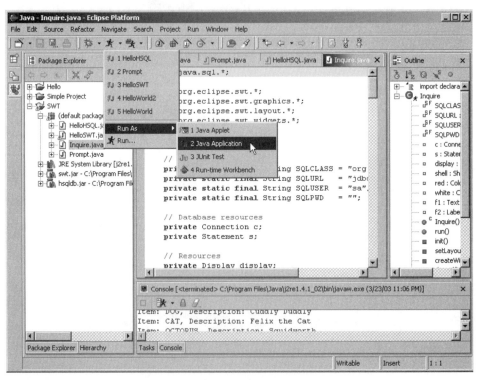

Figure 10.46: Running Inquire as a Java Application.

This will create a launch configuration for Inquire with the default characteristics
and then attempt to run it.

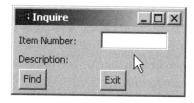

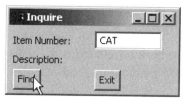

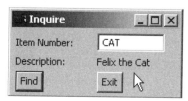

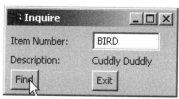

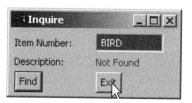

This is the result of the application. The application is functionally the same as the one you created in Step 9. You can enter various values in the Item Number field and click the Find button to see if the value you entered is valid. If it is, you will see a description (the valid item numbers are CAT, DOG, and OCTOPUS).

If you enter an invalid item number, the program will highlight the field as well as returning a value of "Not Found". You can run this as many times as you like. Click the Exit button when you want the application to end.

Congratulations! You have successfully used Eclipse to create and run a Java application incorporating both SWT and JDBC. This is quite an accomplishment.

I hope this book has given you enough insight into the various technologies to continue researching them on your own. Good luck!

For those of you who would care to, I've included a final section reviewing the code for this application. There's really very little changed from the Prompt application in Step 9, and much of what has changed has been covered already in my review of HelloSQL, but it may still be helpful to review the final product.

Code review: Inquire

Most of the code in this method you've seen already, either in the Prompt code (from Step 9) or the HelloSQL application earlier in this step. Since that's the case, I'm only going to highlight and review those lines that you haven't seen before.

```java
import java.sql.*;

import org.eclipse.swt.*;
import org.eclipse.swt.graphics.*;
import org.eclipse.swt.layout.*;
import org.eclipse.swt.widgets.*;

public class Inquire {

        // Database constants
        private static final String sqlClass = "org.hsqldb.jdbcDriver";
        private static final String sqlUrl   = "jdbc:hsqldb:hsqldb";
        private static final String sqlUser  = "sa";
        private static final String sqlPwd   = "";

    // Database resources
    private Connection c;
    private Statement s;

    // Resources
    private Display display;
    private Shell shell;
    private Color red, white;

    // Fields
    private Text f1;
    private Label f2;

    public Inquire() {
    }

    public void run() {
        try {
                init();
                setLayout();
                createWidgets();
                show();
                cleanup();
        }
        catch (Exception e)
        {
                System.out.println("Error: " + e);
        }
    }
```

This is the interesting effect of exceptions. Because some of the lower-level methods now throw exceptions (because they invoke JDBC functions), this high level method must incorporate a try/catch block.

```java
private void init()
        throws Exception
{
        // Open the database
        Class.forName (sqlClass);
        c = DriverManager.getConnection(sqlUrl, sqlUser, sqlPwd);
        s = c.createStatement();

        // Create a standard window
        display = new Display();
        shell = new Shell(display);
        shell.setText("Inquire");
        // Create some colors
        red = new Color(display, 255, 0, 0);
        white = new Color(display, 255, 255, 255);
}
```

This is the other effect of exceptions. Rather than embedding the try/catch in this method, I simply specified a throws clause in the method definition. This will "bubble up" any exceptions to the caller.

```java
private void setLayout() {
        // Create the layout for the widgets
        GridLayout grid = new GridLayout();
        grid.numColumns = 2;
        grid.makeColumnsEqualWidth = true;
        shell.setLayout(grid);
}

private void createWidgets() {
        // Create my widgets
        Label l1 = new Label(shell, SWT.NONE);
        l1.setText("Item Number:");

        f1 = new Text(shell, SWT.BORDER | SWT.SINGLE);
        f1.setTextLimit(20);

        Label l2 = new Label(shell, SWT.NONE);
        l2.setText("Description:");
```

```
        f2 = new Label(shell, SWT.NONE);
        f2.setText(" ";

        Button b1 = new Button(shell, SWT.PUSH);
        b1.setText("Find");
        b1.addListener(SWT.Selection, new Listener() {
            public void handleEvent(Event event) {
                doFind();
            }
        });

        Button b2 = new Button(shell, SWT.PUSH);
        b2.setText("Exit");
        b2.addListener(SWT.Selection, new Listener() {
            public void handleEvent(Event event) {
                doExit();
            }
        });
}
private void doFind()
{
        try {
            String desc = getDescription(f1.getText());
            if (desc == null)
            {
                f1.setForeground(white);
                f1.setBackground(red);
                f2.setText("Not Found");
                f2.setForeground(red);
            }
            else
            {
                f1.setForeground(null);
                f1.setBackground(null);
                f2.setText(desc);
                f2.setForeground(null);
            }
    } catch (Exception e) {
                f1.setForeground(white);
                f1.setBackground(red);
                f2.setText("Error: " + e);
                f2.setForeground(red);
        }
}
```

The doFind method isn't affected too much, except that it must now take exceptions into account. Since the application uses the f2 field to display the "Not Found" message, it made sense to use the same convention to show exception messages.

```
private void doExit() {
      shell.close();
}

private String getDescription(String item)
      throws Exception
{
      String description = null;
      String query = "SELECT * FROM ITEMS WHERE ItemNumber='" + item + "'";
      ResultSet rs = s.executeQuery(query);
      if (rs.next()) description = rs.getString("Description");
      return description;
}
```

The getDescription method is the method most affected by the switch to JDBC. Instead of a hardcoded hash table and a lookup, you must query the database. I'm using the most primitive version of the syntax here: I just format the SELECT statement on the fly. For any but the simplest of queries, this can get very messy, especially when trying to quote strings properly. Instead, you might want to consider a prepared statement (the syntax if which is not covered in this particular manual).

```
private void show() {
      // Final setup - size the display show it
      shell.setSize(200, 100);
      shell.open();
      while (!shell.isDisposed()) {
            if (!display.readAndDispatch())
                  display.sleep();
      }
}

private void cleanup()
      throws Exception
{
```

```
        // When done, clean up resources
        display.dispose();
        red.dispose();
        white.dispose();

        // Shut down database
        s.close();
        c.close();
    }


    public static void main(String[] args) {
        new Inquire().run();
        System.exit(0);
    }
}
```

The only change left is the addition of the throws clause to the cleanup method definition. I'll leave determining the cause for this change as a final exercise for you, my stalwart reader.

I hope you've enjoyed reading this book as much as I've enjoyed writing it!

SideStep 1

Install a Java runtime

GOAL

This is the first SideStep. SideSteps are special chapters designed to help you perform optional steps. In this case, you're going to download the latest Java Virtual Machine (JVM) from Sun. This particular SideStep is for Windows, although the steps are similar for other platforms.

Note: Unlike the main steps, which can get very involved, SideSteps are short and simple. Some don't even have actual instructions, but are more of a discussion of additional areas of research. This first SideStep, however, does have a checklist, as shown on the following page.

✔ **Here is your step checklist:**

❑ S1(a) Browse to java.sun.com.

Figure S1.1: Sun's Java home page, java.sun.com.

Next you have to decide the package to download. The fastest for Windows developers is just to choose the Windows (U.S. English only) JRE download, which is the top one in the list and is the one shown being selected in Figure S1.2. If you would like the Linux version, you can do the same.

Why JRE rather than SDK? Well, it depends on what you plan to do. The JRE is the minimum required to run Java applications. The SDK includes additional utilities that allow you to compile and debug your own Java programs. However, Eclipse is designed to provide all the additional pieces that the SDK provides, and in a single integrated environment to boot. This makes the SDK unnecessary; you only need the much smaller JRE.

❑ **S1(b) Click on the DOWNLOAD link for your platform.**

Figure S1.2: Downloading the JRE only for the Windows version.

❏ **S1(c) Page to the bottom of the license agreement.**

Figure S1.3: Sun's License Agreement for Java.

❑ **S1(d) Click the ACCEPT button.**

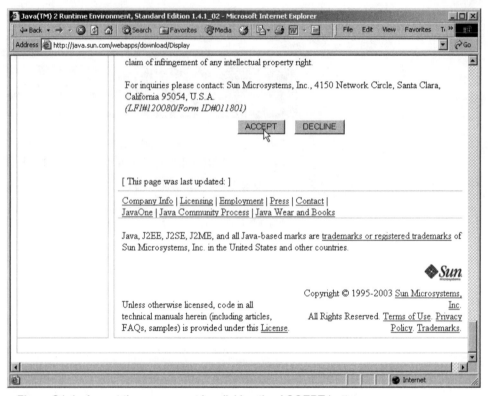

Figure S1.4: Accept the agreement by clicking the ACCEPT button.

❏ **S1(e) Click on the download link.**

Which link shows here will depend upon which option you selected in Step S1(b).

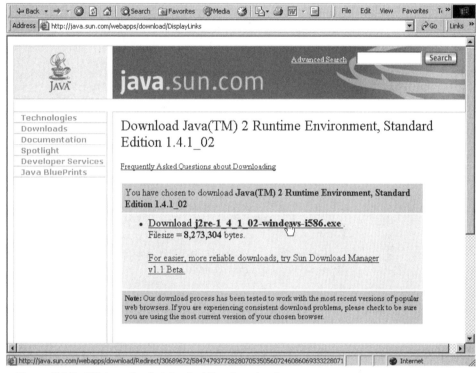

Figure S1.5: Click on the link to start the download.

At this point, you can either save the file someplace on your hard disk, or just download it to a temporary location and run it. I'll show you the quick way:

❑ **S1(f)   Click the Open button, to run the file immediately after download.**

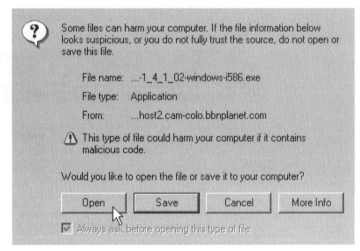

Figure S1.6: Click the Open button—the installer will then be run as soon as it is downloaded.

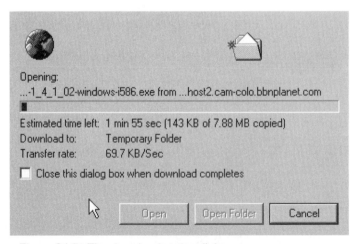

Figure S1.7: The download status dialog.

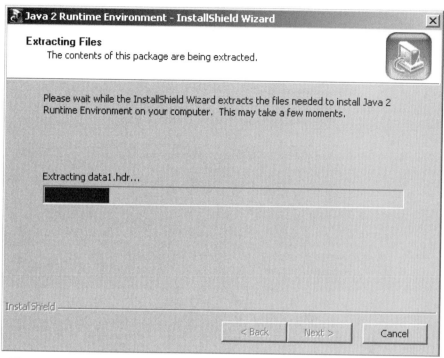

Figure S1.8: The file extraction dialog.

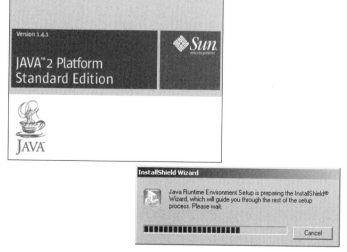

Figure S1.9: The InstallShield startup dialog.

❏ **S1(g) Click Yes to accept the license agreement (again).**

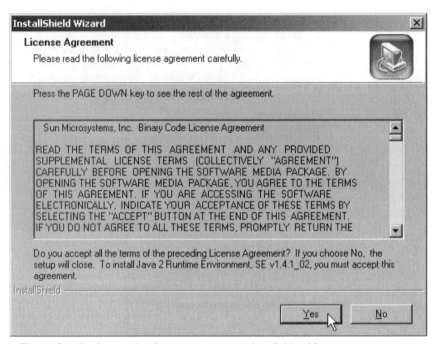

Figure S1.10: Accept the license agreement by clicking Yes.

How you choose to install is up to you, but the easiest way is to perform a "typical" install, which will install the JRE in a folder under C:\Program Files\Java. Don't worry about where; Eclipse will find it.

So just leave "Typical" selected and click Next. You'll see the status display shown in Figure S1.12 and the completion display shown in Figure S1.13, and your brand-new JRE will be installed.

❑ **S1(h) Leave 'Typical' checked and click Next.**

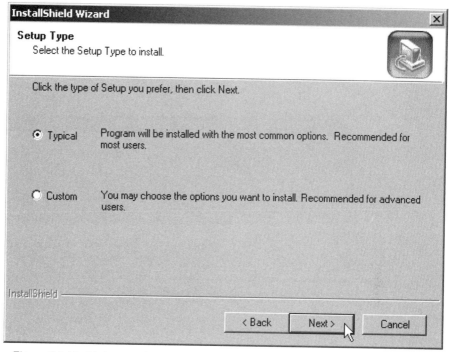

Figure S1.11: Make sure 'typical' is selected and press Next.

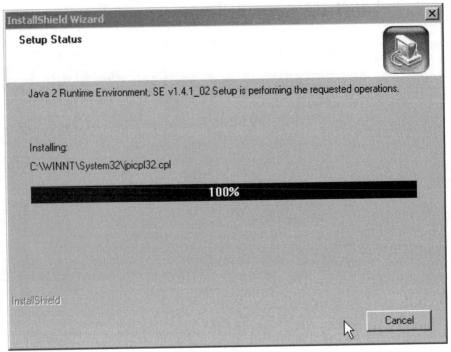

Figure S1.12: The installation status dialog.

Figure S1.13: And you are done.

SideStep 2

Install WinZip

❑ **S2(a) Browse to www.winzip.com.**

❑ **S2(b) Click on Download Evaluation Version.**

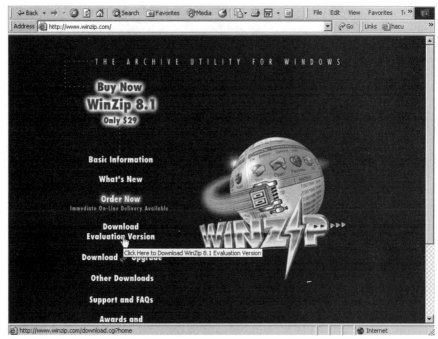

Figure S2.1: Select Download Evaluating Version from the WinZip home page, www.winzip.com.

At this point, you need to select a place to download from. I use CNET, because it's usually very fast and reliable.

❑ **S2(c) Click on a download link.**

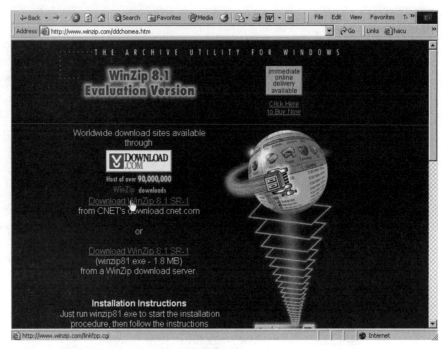

Figure S2.2: Downloading from CNET.

You can download the WinZip installer onto your hard disk and run it, or you can just run it automatically when the download is complete. I'll show you how to do the latter.

❑ **S2(d) When the download dialog pops up, select Open.**

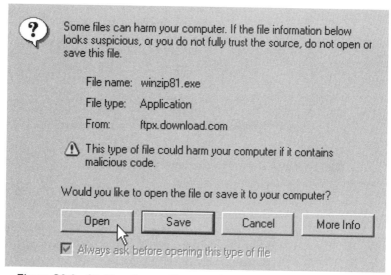

Figure S2.3: Clicking Open will cause the installer to run as soon as it is downloaded.

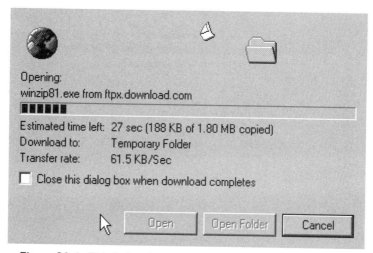

Figure S2.4: This is the download status dialog.

❏ **S2(e) When the installer dialog pops up, click Setup.**

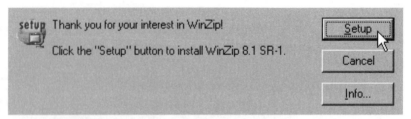

Figure S2.5: Click Setup to begin the installation.

❏ **S2(f) Leave the defaults and click OK.**

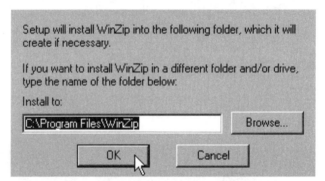

Figure S2.6: Leave the defaults and click OK to install WinZip into C:\Program Files.

Since I'm a supporter of shareware, I actually have a registered copy. Each time I download a new version, I get a screen such as the one following. If you don't have a registered copy, you may not see this screen.

❑ **S2(g) If you have a registered copy, click OK on the registration screen.**

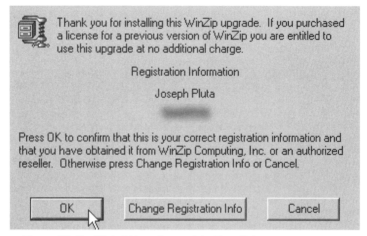

Figure S2.7: Click OK on the registration dialog.

❑ **S2(h) On the installation-complete dialog, click Next.**

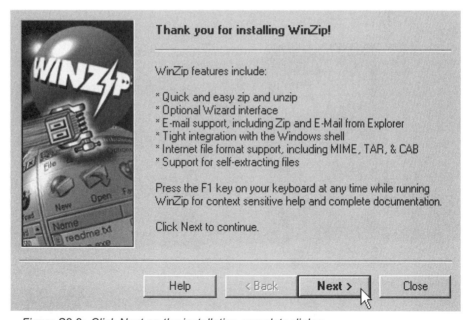

Figure S2.8: Click Next on the installation-complete dialog.

❑ **S2(i) Click Yes to accept the license.**

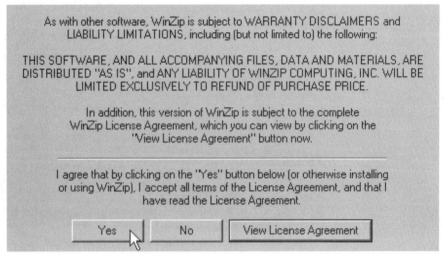

As with other software, WinZip is subject to WARRANTY DISCLAIMERS and
LIABILITY LIMITATIONS, including (but not limited to) the following:

THIS SOFTWARE, AND ALL ACCOMPANYING FILES, DATA AND MATERIALS, ARE
DISTRIBUTED "AS IS", and ANY LIABILITY OF WINZIP COMPUTING, INC. WILL BE
LIMITED EXCLUSIVELY TO REFUND OF PURCHASE PRICE.

In addition, this version of WinZip is subject to the complete
WinZip License Agreement, which you can view by clicking on the
"View License Agreement" button now.

I agree that by clicking on the "Yes" button below (or otherwise installing
or using WinZip), I accept all terms of the License Agreement, and that I
have read the License Agreement.

[Yes]   [No]   [View License Agreement]

Figure S2.9: Click Yes to accept the license.

❑ **S2(j) Click Next on the Quick Start page.**

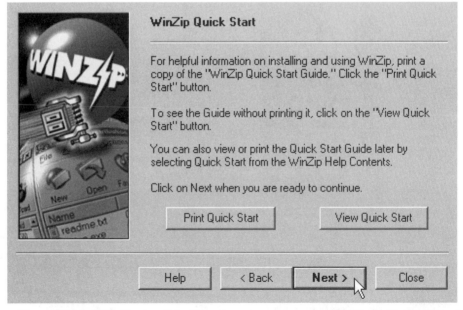

WinZip Quick Start

For helpful information on installing and using WinZip, print a
copy of the "WinZip Quick Start Guide." Click the "Print Quick
Start" button.

To see the Guide without printing it, click on the "View Quick
Start" button.

You can also view or print the Quick Start Guide later by
selecting Quick Start from the WinZip Help Contents.

Click on Next when you are ready to continue.

[Print Quick Start]   [View Quick Start]

[Help]   [< Back]   [**Next >**]   [Close]

*Figure S2.10: Click Next on this dialog (you can always view the Quick Start guide
later).*

I personally prefer WinZip Classic, so I always install it that way.

❏ **S2(k) Select 'Start with WinZip Classic' and click Next.**

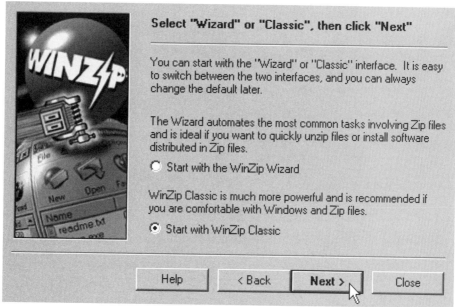

Figure S2.11: Select WinZip Classic and click Next.

Use Express setup; it's fast and easy.

❑ **S2(l) Select 'Express setup' and click Next.**

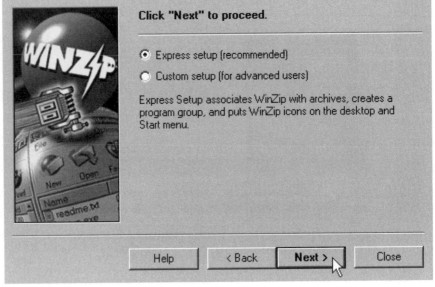

Figure S2.12: Run Express Setup by selecting it and pressing Next.

❑ **S2(m)Click Finish.**

Figure S2.13: After the installation is complete, click Finish.

❑ **S2(n) Click Close on the hint dialog.**

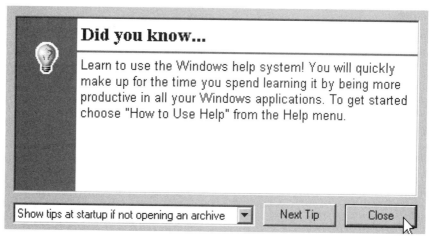

Figure S2.14: Close the hint dialog.

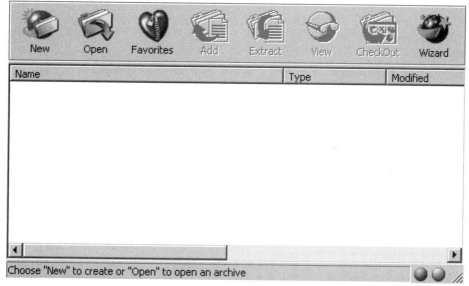

Figure S2.15: The WinZip display appears!

SideStep 3

Download Eclipse

GOAL

In this step, you will download the Eclipse IDE from the Eclipse website. The IDE is downloaded as a ZIP file, which you will store in a temporary folder on your disk drive.[1] You will install the IDE beginning in Step 2.3.

✔ **Here is your step checklist:**

---

[1]Typically in Windows, you will have a folder called My Downloads in the folder My Documents. If you don't, create one. Then create a folder named Eclipse in the My Downloads folder.

❏ S3(a) Browse to the Eclipse Web site.

Downloading Eclipse is one of the easier tasks you'll find in your move to the new GUI development world. I'll walk you through it. First, fire up your favorite browser and point it to www.eclipse.org, as shown in Figure S3.1.

❑ S3(b) Navigate to the downloads page.

The left-hand navigation column has several options, one of which is "downloads." Click on it to go to the downloads page.

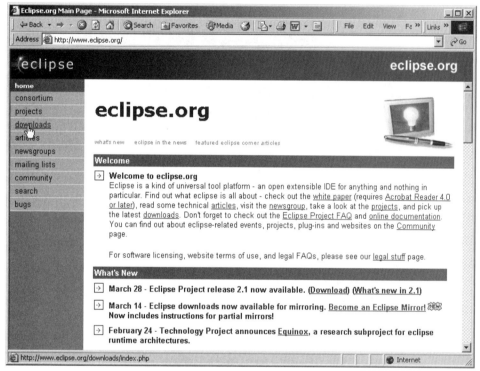

Figure S3.1: The opening page for the Eclipse Web site on April 17, 2003 (just after the release of version 2.1).

The downloads page appears, as shown in Figure S3.2. It contains a list of "mirrors"—sites that have copies of the software for download. In my example, I'll be using the North American mirror, but you can use whichever one is best for you.

❏ **S3(c) Navigate to the appropriate mirror by clicking on it.**

Choose the mirror site best for you geographically, and click on it.

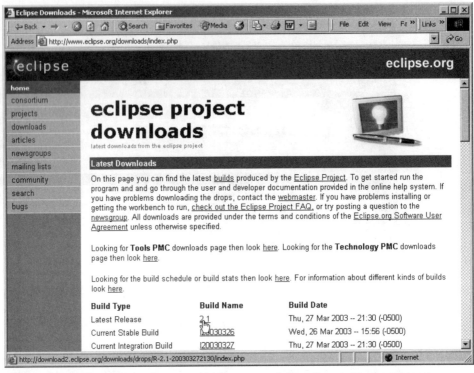

Figure S3.2: The downloads page at Eclipse.org; click on the server closest to you.

Clicking on the desired mirror will bring you to the second downloads page, as shown in Figure S3.3.

❏ S3(d) Select the desired version and navigate to its page.

The second downloads page is the same on every mirror. It will allow you to download different versions and releases of Eclipse, from the last "gold" release to the current nightly build.

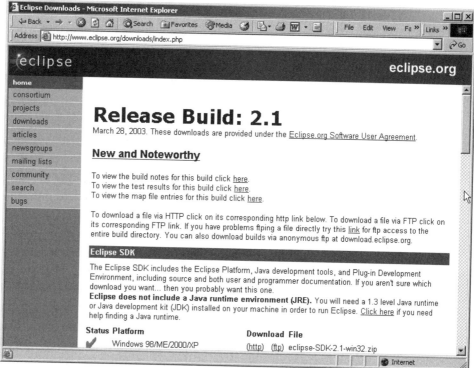

Figure S3.3: The download page at the Eclipse Web site.

The top of the page allows you to download the latest of several types of builds, from the most stable (the release build) to the nightly build, which, as its name suggests, was probably just built the night before and hasn't yet been tested much at all. The more recent the build, the more likely that there are still bugs crawling around.

Eclipse releases come pretty regularly every six months or so, with milestone builds and release candidates in between. The gold releases are listed under a heading "Latest Releases"; if you can't see this heading, scroll down to it. You can also see the milestones and release candidates for this version by scrolling down on this screen to the heading "Current Stable Builds." There you can see items named Mn and RCn. The Mn builds are "milestones": significant function points in the development process, which happen about once a month. The RCn builds are "release candidates": code nearly ready to be pronounced "gold" (that is, made ready for general availability). So, in the life of a release you'll see four or five milestones (M1-M5), followed by three release candidates. Anything before M4 or M5 is subject to pretty drastic change before release date, and even release candidates may see changes if bugs or inconsistencies are found. For production work, I always suggest using the latest gold release, the rationale being that by the time a version gets to release, most of the bugs have been stamped out.

The release of this book was timed to coincide with the gold release of version 2.1. This is not a milestone or even a release candidate build—it is the final release. This version of Eclipse should be good for developers for at least another six months, when the next gold release comes out. Of course, it's up to you to decide how "bleeding edge" you wish to be. You decide that by weighing the importance of stability versus access to new features. You'll be able to determine that balance best for your own particular needs.

To download a version, you first must get to its page. To get to the page for a version, simply click on it. Figure S3.3 shows me clicking on the 2.1 release download. The book was timed so that this release would be available, and is the one I recommend.[2]

You'll see the page as shown in Figure S3.4. There is quite a bit of extraneous stuff at the start of the page; the part that's important to you starts at the very bottom of the page. It'll be easier to see this if you scroll down a page.

---

[2]By the time you read this, new versions may be available. If you like to see newer features, try the Current Stable Build (check the date to make sure it is later than the current gold release). Only intrepid adventurers should try the Integration or Nightly builds, and then only once you've become familiar enough with Eclipse to be able to distinguish broken code from user errors.

❏ **S3(e) Scroll down a page.**

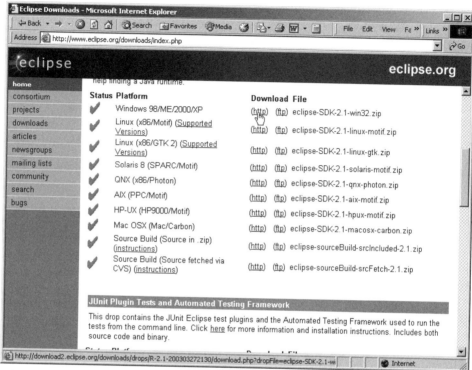

Figure S3.4: The version download page for Release Build 2.1 There is one page for each build version. Roll down a page using the Page Down key on your keyboard or the scroll bar.

You'll see a screen like the one in Figure S3.5. You're not quite done yet. You've picked the version, but you haven't chosen the platform or the components to load. You have several options. You can download the SDK, the Eclipse binary runtime, the JDT binary runtime, and so on. I suggest you start with the SDK, which contains everything including source and documentation. Even if you don't use everything right away, you'll have it all downloaded and available.

❏ S3(f) Select the appropriate file for download.

In this SideStep, I'm going to assume that you're running Windows, so I'll walk you through the Windows download. The Windows version happens to be the top entry, with a link that identifies the file as "eclipse-SDK-2.1-win32.zip." This file name may be different, depending on the release you chose back in the previous step. For example, if you selected release 2.0, you would see "eclipse-SDK-2.0-win32.zip," but the idea is the same.

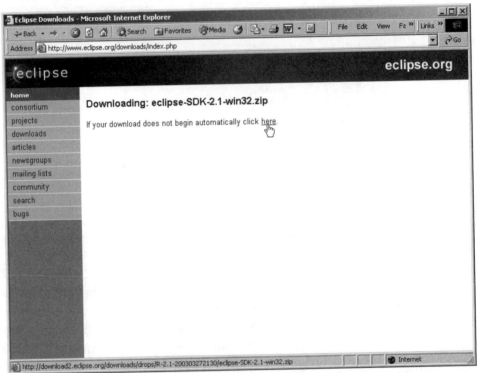

Figure S3.5: The various platforms available for release 2.1. Select the HTTP download of the Windows version.

Your browser will show a page like the one in Figure S3.6. In a few seconds, it should then pop up a dialog like the one in Figure S3.7. If not, click on the link where it says "click here."

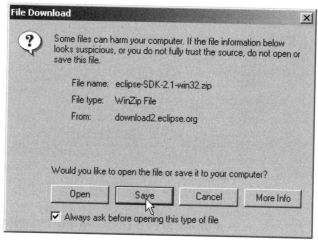

Figure S3.6: Downloading the ZIP file from Eclipse.org. Click on the "click here" link only if the prompt dialog in Figure S3.6 doesn't appear.

You'll eventually get a dialog like the one in Figure S3.7.

❑ **S3(g) Click the Save button.**

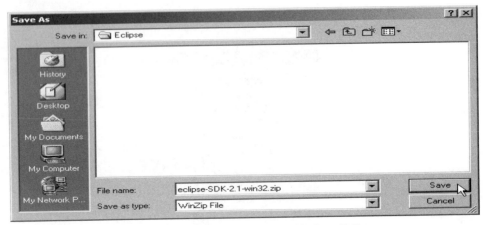

Figure S3.7: Click Save to start downloading the ZIP file from Eclipse.org.

❑ **S3(h) Select a directory to save the ZIP file into.**

Select a directory to save the SDK ZIP file into. I created a separate Eclipse folder under my normal Download folder, since I will be downloading other Eclipse-related software as time goes on.

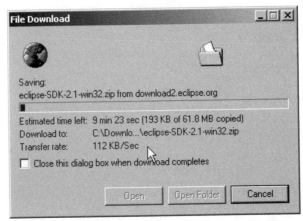

Figure S3.8: Selecting a directory to save the ZIP file into.

You'll see a status dialog like the one in Figure S3.9. Wait for it to complete, and you're done with this SideStep.

❑ **S3(i) Wait for the download to complete.**

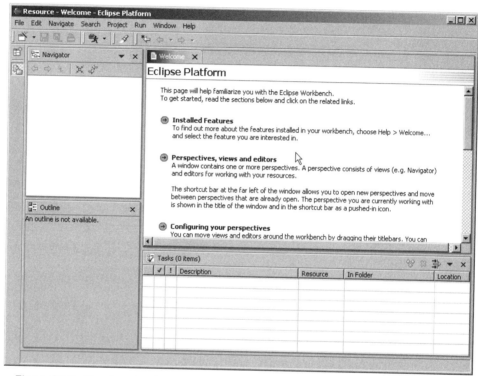

Figure S3.9: The download status box for the SDK.

SideStep 4

**On things
GUI**

GOAL

Learn about the two major competing
graphical user interface (GUI) technologies for Java.

There is no SideStep checklist; I'm just going to talk a little bit about the two different GUIs, Swing and SWT. Both are thick-client user interface (UI) strategies; if your application calls for a browser-based approach, or if you are writing distributed applications and your UI is not written in Java, then this SideStep is purely informational.

The two techniques are conceptually similar: You create widgets of one type or another, which you place on the screen, in areas called panes or panels or canvases or frames. Widgets and their containers can be resized, moved, hidden, and made visible. There are a wide variety of text capabilities, including fonts and colors. You can include background colors and images and even draw your own controls line by line or pixel by pixel.

Both Swing and SWT are event driven, with a dispatcher loop that listens for user requests. These can be anything from button clicks to keystrokes to mouse movements. You can attach listeners to widgets to scan for specific events and take the appropriate actions. This is the design philosophy behind all event-driven user interfaces, and it is what makes them so responsive to the user.

However, beyond those basic characteristics, the two approaches quickly diverge. Even the simplest things are different in the two approaches, and the architectural differences are enormous. Hopefully, after reading this SideStep, you'll be in a position to decide which UI technology best suits your needs.

Here are a couple of good URLs for more information:

- java.sun.com/products/jfc/—Sun's Web site on the Java Foundation Classes, including Swing

- eclipsewiki.swiki.net/2—This is pretty much the only place on the Internet for information on the SWT

There are hundreds of other Websites that deal with Swing, as well as dozens of books. Unfortunately, there are no other Web sites and no books on SWT; this is part of the problem of using a new technology.

Swing—The "Classic" Java UI

Swing is the standard Java UI included with the Java SDK. It has been part of Java since the earliest days, when it superseded the older AWT (Abstract Window Toolkit). The AWT was designed to use "heavyweight" components—this term indicated that the AWT routines directly called OS-specific graphical routines. For example, on Windows, the AWT directly interfaced with the Windows APIs. Various problems arose from this, the top two being the following:

1. Not all operating systems supported the same low-level functions. This meant that code had to be written to support certain functions or, in severe cases, that certain functionality had to be left out of a platform implementation.

2. OS APIs tended to change from version to version. This was particularly true back in the late 1990s, when it seemed that Microsoft was releasing a new operating system every six months. The APIs were wildly inconsistent from one version of the OS to another, and this meant rewriting the AWT interfaces.

With those two objections in mind, the decision was made to switch to a completely "lightweight" implementation of the GUI, and thus Swing was born. I'm not sure of the exact details, but the idea is that only a couple of basic features of the operating system are used, such as creating a window, capturing an event, or drawing simple graphics. Everything else is written in 100% Java. So, when you decide to create a button on the screen, every edge and every line is drawn by the Swing toolkit. If you take the time to look at the buttons on today's GUIs, you'll see that this is actually a pretty complex feat, since the buttons tend to be "three-dimensional," with lighter shading to the left and above and darker shading to the right and below. Not only that, the buttons actually "depress" when you click them. This is quite a bit of work, and with Swing this work is done in Java rather than by the operating system.

This leads to one of the biggest detractions from Swing: its performance. Swing is noticeably slower, especially on smaller machines. While optimizing compilers can help to reduce some of that overhead, Swing to date just hasn't been able to provide as crisp a user interface as native graphics, and this more than anything has slowed its acceptance.

There are many great benefits to Swing. Swing was designed from the ground up to provide complete accessibility for alternate user interface devices, thus allowing applications to be easily modified to support speech- or sight-challenged users or other users with alternate input devices. Swing can also easily change its "look and feel" from one style to another with a single API call, allowing it to switch from mimicking Windows to mimicking the Mac user interface. However, for several reasons, not the least of which is the constant changes in the various operating systems, Swing, while often coming close to the actual look and feel of a native application, never quite accomplishes it.

SWT—The Challenger

Thus enters SWT, the Software Widget Toolkit. SWT is, in some ways, a throwback to the old days of AWT, because SWT is designed to use the native operating system graphical APIs for drawing most of its basic widgets. Although SWT adds support for higher-level concepts such as layout managers, the lower-level SWT widgets rely upon the native OS APIs for their functions.

Unlike the original Swing, which was designed in something of a vacuum without a whole lot of practical application, SWT has been designed in conjunction with its primary application, the Eclipse workbench. And while there is some debate over whether the look and feel of SWT has enough advantage in speed and "native feel" to justify it, there's no doubt that the interface is quite successful in supporting a major development effort.

There are a few differences in basic programming, some subtle, some not so subtle, but the general concepts are quite similar. You create containers and put widgets in them, optionally using layouts to determine the position of those widgets. You can attach listeners to the widgets, written to respond to user actions. Some of the interfaces definitely can be seen to be second generation, in that they build upon and improve their counterparts from the Swing API. Others are simply different, and some are actually more difficult. One of the biggest gripes is that many of the resources you allocate during SWT programming—things such as windows and colors—must be managed by the programmer. Failure to return these resources to the system can cause memory leaks. This is diametrically opposed to the Java concept of garbage collection, and it is a common problem when directly accessing the native OS.

Moreover, there is a very fundamental difference in deployment. For each operating system, you must include a native library, such as a DLL in Windows or a shared library in Linux. This native library is constantly evolving, so you must include the correct one for your version of SWT with your application. Any operating system that does not have a native library cannot run SWT applications. And while the SWT development team seems to be making every effort to support a wide variety of operating systems, this is just one more piece of OS-specific software you need to worry about.

So, the tradeoff is simple: a more native, more responsive look and feel, or a more portable but perhaps less powerful API. You'll need to make your decision based on your business requirements, but hopefully I've given you some information to help you make that decision.

The Swing Source

I thought it was important that any book that deals with Eclipse should also deal with SWT, since SWT is the underlying user interface for Eclipse. Makes sense, eh? Not only that, there was no real tutorial on using Swing and Eclipse together, and as I found, it's not exactly intuitive.

So, all the primary examples in the book use SWT as the interface. This is not meant to be an opinion as to whether SWT is better than Swing or vice versa; it is simply the decision made when selecting the content of the book.

However, I know that some of you may be familiar with Swing and may prefer it. Alternately, some of you may have no idea whatsoever what Swing is and may want to see some examples of Swing code. To that end, I have included Swing versions of the various graphical application in this book, as follows:

Step	Example	UI	Location
9	HelloSWT	SWT	/Source/Step 9/HelloSWT.java
	HelloSwing	Swing	/Source/Step 9 (Swing)/HelloSwing.java
9	Prompt	SWT	/Source/Step 9/Prompt.java
	PromptSwing	Swing	/Source/Step 9 (Swing)/PromptSwing.java
10	Inquire	SWT	/Source/Step 10/Inquire.java
	InquireSwing	Swing	/Source/Step 10 (Swing)/InquireSwing.java

There were two thick-client applications in Step 9 and one in Step 10. The examples in the book are all SWT. For each SWT example there is a corresponding Swing example. All code for both UI types is on the included CD-ROM.

SideStep 5

Start your SQL engines

GOAL

Get an introduction
to some other freeware SQL engines.

I included HSQLDB as the database for this book because it is Open Source and 100% Pure Java. Open Source makes it possible for programmers to learn new technologies on their own. 100% Pure Java means that this database will run anywhere a JVM runs, so certainly it will run wherever Eclipse runs. But that doesn't mean it's the only valid database. You should research various databases and find out which suits your needs. Use this SideStep as a starting point.

This is a very short SideStep. I don't plan to provide much more information than links to the website for the various SQL engines I've found. However, I would like to point out something. Of all the databases I found, only IBM's JTOpen (which connects to an iSeries database) and SAP's SAP DB database provide comprehensive support for the new JDBC 2.0 specification. The others support only the minimum JDBC 2.0 requirements, and provide no implementation of what I consider to be the most important addition to the standard: scrollable, updatable cursors.

Without going into a long diatribe, scrollable, updatable cursors allow applications to position themselves within and through a view a record at a time and perform updates on records only if the application decides such an update is necessary. The business logic used to determine what updates need to be performed does not have to adhere to SQL syntax and can instead be of any arbitrary complexity. This sort of flexibility is crucial to business applications and makes SQL far more useful for implementing complex business rules.

Anyway, I've provided the basic HelloHSQL program in each of three additional dialects, all located in the folder /Source/Step 10 (Other DB). It's pretty easy to switch form one database to another programmatically; the setup is a little more difficult. More information on all four of the databases can be found at the following URLs:

- HSQLDB—a 100% Pure Java SQL database: hsqldb.sourceforge.net/

- JTOpen (JT/400)—IBM's Open Source Java Toolbox for the iSeries (AS/400): www-124.ibm.com/developerworks/oss/jt400/index.html

- PostgreSQL—one of the most popular Open Source SQL packages: www.postgresql.org/

- SAP DB—the free version of SAP's very robust database: www.sapdb.org/

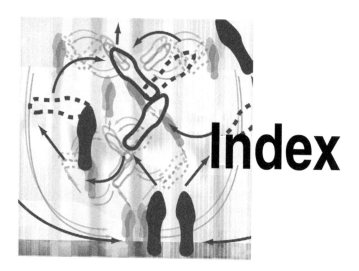

Index

Note: Boldface numbers indicate illustrations.

Note: Boldface numbers indicate illustrations.

Note: Boldface numbers indicate illustrations.

Note: Boldface numbers indicate illustrations.